Right Social Justice

Better ways to help the poor

GARY JOHNS - EDITOR

connorcourt
PUBLISHING

Published in Australia by Connor Court Publishing 2012

Connor Court Publishing Pty Ltd
PO Box 1
Ballan VIC 3342
sales@connorcourt.com
www.connorcourt.com

ISBN 978-1-921421-62-4

Cover design by Ian James

Printed in Australia

**Connor Court Publishing Pty Ltd and
Australian Catholic University Public Policy Institute Series
in
Government, Policy and Politics**

Series editor:
Professor Scott Prasser,
Executive Director, Public Policy Institute, Australian Catholic University

*A series of research, books, articles, seminars, roundtables and
conferences that seeks to explore Australia's past, present and future
developments in government, policy and politics.*

*ACU's Public Policy Institute seeks to inform public debate through
research, commentary and analysis on current issues and active engagement with the broader community through a wide range of forums.*

Table of Contents

Does social justice help the poor?

Gary Johns

Social justice has worked its way into the lexicon of social policy. Few, however, understand its meaning or implications for public policy. The concept has very little explanatory power. It cannot, for example, explain who is to pay to assist the poor, how poor one has to be to be eligible for assistance or, indeed, at what point no further assistance should be offered. In short, social justice is a belief, not a guide to public policy.

To help devotees of social justice, and others who may wish to understand more of its impact on public policy, I have asked some of the best observers of the welfare state in Australia and its associated programs to contribute to a volume exploring the concept. Each was asked to consider the dominant view of social justice in their chosen field. Each was encouraged to provide a quote from the advocates for such a view. Their challenge was to respond to the dominant view and provide a better way to help 'the poor'. They have responded with insightful and erudite papers. The results will open the field to fresh, rigorous examination of social policy.

Most writers are of liberal frame of mind. They question the right of government to decide our fate. Others are more disposed to the welfare state yet question the current plethora of programs developed in the name of 'doing good'. They, too, think that there are better ways to help the poor.

Many a student of the social sciences has had to suffer lectures about how fair European social democracies are by comparison with Australia. Now that much of southern Europe is looking decidedly ill, falling prey to governments that cannot balance their budgets, such lecturers may have cause to reassess. In reassessing, however, they need not overthrow the idea of social justice as an economy-wide determinant of the distribution of wealth. They do need to appreciate better that so long as people freely give their permission, any number of redistributions of wealth can be held to be just.

Social justice does not provide a definitive template for redistribution of wealth because democratically elected representatives have learned that their constituents do not share the same values. Moreover, in striving to satisfy many differing views of what is a just distribution, unintended consequences arise. One is creation of a culture that lacks the discipline necessary to manage, in a sustainable way, transfers between different classes of citizen – hence the southern European phenomenon. Another is to make individuals overly reliant on government thus helping to create the very condition social justice seeks to ameliorate.

By and large, Australia has managed income transfers in a sustainable way, but, as the welfare state grows, it runs the risk of creating the scourge of the southern European culture – that the citizen exists for the state and not the state for the citizen. Measured by income distribution, Australia is a socially just society by comparison with all others. This is not to argue that more should not be done for the poor as wealth and forbearance provides, but that social justice as a philosophy fails to indicate how much more. It fails to specify the point at which social justice has been achieved. Neither does it acknowledge failings and risks.

The Gillard Government, for example, is simultaneously considering very expensive proposals for a national disability insurance scheme, a national dental scheme, further schools funding, especially to the disadvantage, and a national mental health scheme. At the same time it has built school halls across Australia, without allocating money for maintenance, power and cleaning. It has supplied students with laptops without allocating money to service them. Funding every known problem, without priority and without taking into account the ongoing expenses is foolhardy. But the foolhardiness has been encouraged by the ideology of social justice which provides no guide to difficult choices.

Who should come first and by how much, which problem is to be treated first and for how long? Governments every day face these problems, but they have precious little guidance to solve them. Perhaps the advocates for social justice have work to do after all, but I doubt they know where to start.

Our suggestion for a starting point is acceptance that democratic polities and a substantial majority of people agree to order society in ways that redistribute wealth toward the less well off. There is, however, a liberal's wariness of the very idea of an ideal society-wide distribution and the expanding rationale for it. Questioning the extent of redistribution, its impact on the production of the surplus, and the effectiveness of government programs developed in the name of social justice is a good thing. Above all, it is important to suggest better ways to assist the poor and recognize that there may never be 'enough policy levers'[1] to put everything right.

The book is organised in two parts.

The first consists of four thematic longer essays. These pose some fundamental questions about social justice realized in the welfare state. The first essay, 'When too much social justice is never enough', notes the strong transfers of wealth between income classes in Australia, but questions the degree of support for the egalitarian concept of social justice. The second essay, 'The welfare state grows and grows', by Julie Novak, describes the long run growth, reach and magnitude of the welfare state and notes the contributions to its growth from both major political parties in Australia. She questions the future of the welfare state, in particular its diminution of individual responsibility and freedom of action.

In the third essay, 'Are equal societies better societies?' Peter Saunders comprehensively rebuts the oft-supported arguments of egalitarians that equal societies are better than unequal ones. It may come as a shock to egalitarians, but the data relied upon by their champions is without substance. The fourth essay, 'When to stop government programs' by Cassandra Wilkinson, raises the problem that programs persist long after they have proven ineffective because politicians fail to withstand the pressure from 'disadvantaged' recipients and more particularly their advocates, to continue them.

The second part of the book consists of ten shorter essays. Each canvasses a particular program or policy aimed to assist the

---

1 Deborah Cobb-Clark, 'Disadvantage Across the Generations: What Do We Know About Social and Economic Mobility in Australia?' *Economic Record*. 2010, 86(1), 17.

disadvantaged.

Wesley Aird argues that the 'Closing the Gap' policy designed to address the gap between Aborigines and non-Aborigines employs a strategy that is itself not socially just. 'Closing the Gap' creates a false division along racial lines and expects Aboriginal people in need to attend their local Aboriginal-specific organization, to 'engage in the theatre of consultation', and to receive so-called 'culturally appropriate' services. Such divisions are part of the problem.

Child protection is a difficult issue for those who place a premium on limited state intrusion into the lives of individuals. Child protection reform that upholds the independent rights of children is, argues Jeremy Sammut, nevertheless essential because 'we live in a world the Right did not make'. Restoring the role of the Right means asking people to spend time in meetings arguing with Leftists who think the drug-addled have a right to raise children 'with appropriately funded support services.' The reality is: dysfunctional parents damage their children.

Ruth Limkin asserts that 'the receipt of welfare alone has failed to alleviate poverty and disadvantage, particularly for children of welfare-dependent households'. Her experience tells her, though, that there is a particular strength in faith organisations in mobilising community responses to disadvantage. 'Faith organisations have an existing membership that is already engaged, and a leadership and communication structure that enhances the capacity to respond effectively to need'. It is little wonder, she argues, that even dedicated governments compare poorly with these 'sophisticated local networks' in enhancement of community development and provision of service delivery.

Grace Collier examines the Commonwealth's Fair Dismissal Code, contending that employers are starting to realise that no one can resign, or be made redundant without the prospect of an unfair dismissal claim. She proposes a 'no-fault' dismissal system. The underlying principle would be that any governmental intervention into an 'employment separation' must be a worthwhile intervention that provides genuine assistance to those who authentically need it.

In foreign aid the road to hell is paved with good intentions. To avoid the pitfalls, Peter Urban believes that poverty reduction should be left to the International Monetary Fund and that responsibility for aid policy and programs should be transferred from AusAID to the Treasury. Existing bilateral aid should be refocused away from poverty toward social justice, where social justice is centred upon the individual and their access to adequate sustenance, housing and water; to live within a sustainable environment; and to have access to health care.

One of few points of health policy consensus between Australia's progressive Left and the liberal-conservative Right is that prevention of illness and injury is far better and cheaper than cure. The question Terry Barnes poses is: who is responsible for preventable disease? He proposes that a workable Australian individual-responsibility approach in health would require some sort of 'mutual obligation contract' under which a person is given support in return for pursuing positive health behaviours.

Asher Judah traces the 'remarkable transformation' of welfare obligations in Australia during the past century, a transition from an era without any tests to one entirely defined by them. Through a process of trial and error, the evolution of welfare obligations has shown that liberty and compassion alone are 'not enough to overpower the seductiveness of welfare without responsibility'. Only the imposition of obligations, backed by threat of sanctions, has been successful in achieving lasting change based upon the principle that all Australians are entitled to welfare support when circumstances demand it.

Mirko Bagaric considers that nearly all immigration to western countries, including Australia, is based on what immigrants can do for the country. Hence countries readily admit highly skilled people who can add value to the economic infrastructure of the country and cashed-up tourists who inject money directly into the local economy. Refugee settlement standards are different. They are based on compassion. Bagaric believes that the grounds on which the United Nations *Convention Relating to the Status of Refugees* is based should be abolished. Instead, people should be treated equally not on the basis of the *reason* for the persecution, but by *the extent of the need* for asylum.

Sinclair Davidson recalls Milton Friedman's description of the introduction of the welfare state in Germany of the 1880s as a combination of 'paternalism and shrewd politics'. While the shrewd politics has remained, paternalism as the underlying rationale for welfare has changed. Now an argument for 'egalitarianism' or 'equity' underpins welfare. In Davidson's view, provision of 'social justice' via the welfare system remains shrewd politics and provides for massive redistribution while doing little for the actual poor.

These essays provide the basis for a major reconsideration of social justice as a rationale for the welfare state. It is the right time to ask if there are better ways to help the poor and, indeed, if there are enough policy levers to put everything right.

I would like to thank Anthony Cappello of Connor Court and Scott Prasser of the Public Policy Institute, Australian Catholic University, for their support in the project. Also, thanks to John Nethercote of the PPI for his excellent editing. Special thanks goes to each of the 12 contributors who, I believe, have given pause for thought.

Brisbane
March 2012

1
When too much social justice is never enough

Gary Johns

If some individuals benefit from a social process which pushes others below the benchmark, compensation is owed.[2]

Australia is a socially just society

The classical liberal, F. A. Hayek, would, no doubt, be turning in his grave if he were to observe the amount of 'social justice' undertaken in Australia. By contrast, advocates of social justice too numerous to name would argue that social justice has not been achieved in Australia nor elsewhere.[3] Those same advocates, however, would be hard pressed to be definitive about its achievement. After upwards of 50 years of the welfare state, one might ask, are we there yet? To borrow a phrase, 'when too much social justice is never enough', is a reminder of the elastic nature of social justice.

Hayek understood social justice as a synonym for distributive or, indeed, redistributive justice. People who argue for social justice seek to reassign income from the wealthy to the poor throughout an entire society and generally applying to economic or other resources as well as institutions and rules affecting life chances. Hayek sought a society which demanded just action by individuals, while the society which satisfies the demands for social justice, he argued, 'places the duty of justice on authorities with power to command people what to

---

2 D. Harris, *Justifying State Welfare*. Oxford: Basil Blackwell, 1987, 163.
3 The concept is so widespread that for example the United Nations Secretary-General issues an annual *Message for World Day of Social Justice* each February 20.

do.'[4] Hayek was, by and large, thinking of socialist societies. Hayek abhorred socialism, but he thought it impossible that any society 'could organize ... in a manner which makes it possible to assign particular shares of the product of society to the different individuals or groups.'[5] Hayek was sceptical about the motives of those who advocate 'social justice', believing that it is often linked to spurious claims to moral superiority. He railed that social justice had become the 'the chief outlet for moral emotion, the distinguishing attribute of the good man, and the recognized sign of the possession of a moral conscience'. He observed its embrace by Christians who, 'while increasingly losing their faith in a supernatural revelation, appear to have sought a refuge and consolation in a new "social" religion which substitutes a temporal for a celestial promise of justice'.[6]

Nevertheless, whatever classical liberals may wish, it is clear that liberal democratic societies, including Australia, choose to organise in ways that redistribute the shares of the products of society. Liberals would readily acknowledge that people freely choosing to share the surplus is an entirely reasonable activity, but they are also wary of the ability of the majority to take the legitimately acquired resources from the minority. Australians choose to reassign income in large measure through their voluntary effort, either directly or through not-for-profit institutions, or through government benefits and taxes. The system of government benefits and taxes in Australia, for example, means that low income households receive more social benefits in cash and social transfers in kind and pay less tax than high income households. The net effect of benefits and taxes is to increase the average income of households in lower income groups, and decrease the average income of households in higher income groups. A recent government study found that the net effect of benefits and taxes in Australia was to increase the average income of households in the lowest income group from $31

4 F. A. Hayek, 'Social or Distributive Justice.' In *Law, Legislation and Liberty*. Routledge and Kegan Paul, 1982, volume 2, 66.
5 Hayek, 1982, 64.
6 Hayek, 1982, 64.

per week to $479 per week.[7] In the highest group, the net effect was to decrease income from $1623 per week to $1168 per week.[8]

Table 1 shows clearly the redistribution of income from high to low income households.[9] The highest private income quintile paid 46.7 percent of the taxes but received 9 percent of benefits; the lowest quintile paid 5.6 percent of the taxes and received 41.1 percent of the benefits. Within the lowest private income quintile, the share of income received by households increased from 0.9 percent using the private income measure to 13.2 percent using the final income measure (includes benefits). For households in the highest quintile, the income share decreased from 45.7 percent for private income to 32.1 percent for final income.[10]

Measures of economic well-being,[11] which include not only the consumption of householders, but also consumption of non-profit institutions serving households, such as churches, social and sporting clubs and associations (but excludes the free or subsidised consumption of services by households, such as for health and education), suggest that for the bottom 40 percent of the income distribution, these subsidised goods and services increase after tax incomes and their consumption possibilities by about 50 percent. Whether through direct voluntary deeds,[12] or through the not-for-profit sector, which is substantially

7 Australian Bureau of Statistics, *Government Benefits, Taxes and Household Income Australia 2003-04*, No. 6537.0, 2007, 11. Of the total Commonwealth, state and local government taxation revenue in 2003-04, the study allocates 59 percent of total government revenue (net of the subsidies). Of total government expenditure the study allocates benefits of 51 percent of total government expenditure. The unallocated amounts mainly reflect taxation and government expenditure that are not conceptually relatable to individual households, but they also reflect the lack of suitable indicators on which to allocate some taxation revenue, such as capital gains tax, and some benefits.

8 Updated to 2010 to account for inflation using the Reserve Bank of Australia Inflation calculator.

9 Equivalised private income quintile groups are formed by ranking households based on the level of their private income, after adjusting for the size and composition of the household. ABS, 2007, 79.

10 ABS, 2007, 11.

11 Australian Bureau of Statistics, 'Real Final Household Sector Consumption Expenditure.' No. 1370.0 – *Measures of Australia's Progress*, 2010.

12 There are 4.6 million Australian volunteers. Productivity Commission, *Contribution of the Not-for-Profit Sector*, Australian Government, 2010, 67.

assisted by government,[13] or through taxes and benefits, Australians provide social justice on a scale befitting Hayek's worst nightmare.

Table 1.
Distribution of household income, benefits and taxes, Australia 2003-04

Equivalised Private Income Quintile	Lowest Quintile (%)	Highest Quintile (%)	All (Quintiles) Households (%)
Taxes	5.6	46.7	100
Benefits	41.1	9.0	100
Private income	0.9	45.7	100
Final income	13.2	32.1	100

Source: Australian Bureau of Statistics, *Government Benefits, Taxes and Household Income Australia 2003-04, 6537.0*. 2007, *Table 5, 12*.

Either as a result of such substantial redistribution or for reasons associated with Australian culture and society, Australia's poor fare well in international comparisons. Australia is a wealthy country.[14] It is better to be poor in Australia than most other places in the world. For example, using the Gini coefficient,[15] which provides a single statistical measure of the degree of income inequality (which is not a measure of absolute poverty), Australia is close to the OECD average.[16] Nevertheless, in 1997-98 the Gini coefficient was 0.303 compared with 0.331 in 2007-08, representing an increase of 9.2 percent.[17] An analogous OECD study suggested that the poverty rate for Australia rose from 11 percent

---

13 Australian governments provide a range of tax concessions to eligible not-for-profit organisations. The value of deductible gifts claimed by Australian taxpayers on individual income tax returns was over $1.8 billion in 2006-07, with an estimated cost to tax revenue (tax expenditure) of $860 million. Productivity Commission, *Contribution of the Not-for-Profit Sector*, Australian Government, 2010, 155.
14 World Bank, *GNI Per Capita*.
15 The Gini coefficient lies between 0 and 1, with perfect equality at zero and income inequality increasing as the Gini coefficient approaches 1.
16 OECD, *Growing Unequal? Income Distribution and Poverty in OECD Countries*. 2008, figure 1.1.
17 ABS, 2010.

of the total population to 12 percent in the period, 1994 to 2003.[18] In relative terms, Australia's poor appeared to be slipping backwards in the period.

This figure, however, is misleading. What the OECD study did not reveal is that between 1997-98 and 2007-08 the real income of low income households in Australia increased by around 40 percent.[19] The same OECD study showed that a number of European countries – for example, Spain, Portugal and Greece – were more egalitarian than Australia; they had lower proportions of those living in 'relative' poverty but their incomes had not risen as quickly as those in Australia (nor were they as wealthy to begin with).[20] The poor of Spain, Portugal and Greece have often swapped their European egalitarianism for a fair slice of the Australian pie.

Nor did the OECD study show that these 'egalitarian' countries had substantial 'shadow economies'.[21] In other words, people were not paying taxes. There are two possible explanations for non-payment of taxes. It could be a revolt by the middle classes at the level of tax imposed by government as it seeks to achieve the desired level of redistribution.[22] Alternatively, it may be a sign among people who, at one and the same time, demand pensions but do not want to pay for them. One of the consequences of too great tax imposition or too shallow taxpayers' morality is the enormous public debt that these and other countries have accumulated – a clear case of when too much social justice is never enough.

More disconcertingly, it suggests that the egalitarian ethos underpinning social justice is not necessarily built on moral foundations. These countries cannot afford the levels of pensions and benefits they pay. And yet all sorts of claims are made about how the welfare state is of a higher moral order. There is evidence, in fact, that the reason for the behaviour of citizens is deeply cultural, precedes establishment of

---

18 OECD, 2008.
19 ABS, 2010.
20 OECD, 2008, figure 1.1.
21 Friedrich Schneider, 'The Increase of the Size of the Shadow Economy of 18 OECD Countries: Some Preliminary Explanations.' CESifo *Working Paper Series*. 2000, 18.
22 Matthew Fleming, John Roman and Graham Farrell, 'The Shadow Economy.' *Journal of International Affairs*. Spring 2000, 53(2), 394.

the welfare state, and has little to do with conscious achievement of distributive justice.[23]

While measures of relative poverty are common and popular among social justice advocates (they ensure that 'poverty will always be with us'), they can prove very costly and ultimately harmful for the poor by masking other more important causes of poverty, relative or otherwise.[24] Measures of inequality, including relative poverty, are not the sole determinant of how the poor fare. It is as important to know whether there are opportunities to escape poverty. Within one generation in Australia the same individuals were not necessarily in the low income group for the entire period 1997-98 and 2007-08. Through changed circumstances some of the households that had relatively low income in 1997-98 had moved up the income distribution by 2007-08. Others may have slipped into this group, perhaps by retiring and moving to an age pension, by losing their job, or because the death of a partner has reduced total household income. For those who did remain in the low income group, however, their rising income would, on average, have provided a capacity to increase their standard of living.[25] There were also opportunities to escape poverty after one generation. Using estimates of intergenerational earnings for Australian fathers and sons,[26] and intergenerational correlation in educational attainment,[27] for example, it is clear that mobility across generations in Australia is high. Australia ranks in the company of OECD countries such as Finland, Canada, Sweden and Germany, which have substantially higher intergenerational earnings mobility than do countries such as Italy, the United States and the United Kingdom.[28]

It is highly probable that Australian society will remain at the present

23 Andreas Bergh and Christian Bjørnskov, 'Historical Trust Levels Predict the Current Size of the Welfare State.' *Kyklos*. 2011, 64(1).

24 Norman Dennis, *The Invention of Permanent Poverty*. London: The Institute of Economic Affairs. 1998.

25 ABS, 2010.

26 Andrew Leigh 'Intergenerational Mobility in Australia.' *The B.E. Journal of Economic Analysis & Policy*. 2007, 7(2), 18.

27 Deborah Cobb-Clark, 'Disadvantage across the Generations: What Do We Know about Social and Economic Mobility in Australia?' *Economic Record*. 2010, 86(1), 17.

28 Anna Cristina D'Addio, 'Intergenerational Transmission of Disadvantage: Mobility or Immobility Across Generations? A Review of the Evidence for OECD Countries.' *OECD Social, Employment and Migration Working Papers*. 2007, 52, 4.

level of inequality for the foreseeable future. That is, there will not be any significant shift in the relative income and earnings of the upper and lower income quintiles and that the proportions of money that flow progressively from upper to lower will also remain stable. More importantly, Australia's poor and disadvantaged are better off than those in most other societies and their prospects are improving along with those of all other Australians. Furthermore, unlike those in many other countries, Australian redistributions are financially sustainable.

Ambit claims and rules of thumb

Australia has arrived at its level of redistribution for a number of reasons. First, and perhaps foremost, the redistribution is a result of what Australians believe to be a fair reward for their labours operating through both the wages and taxation systems. Second, and closely associated with belief in fair reward, the redistribution is a result of what Australians believe is a fair arrangement for those less fortunate. Their belief will probably be based on a mixture of altruism or 'Christian duty', origins of which extend to the Poor laws in 19th century England, and social insurance, origins of which extend to Bismarck's 19th century Germany, based on an assessment of the risk of falling into poverty. In addition, prominent formulations of 'the just society' would also influence continuing policy debate in Australia.

The rationale for the transfer of income and wealth between citizens is contested ground, broadly between liberals (in political terms, the Right) and progressives (the Left). Liberals are wary of the amount of money transferred between citizens, its impact on those who contribute the funds, and sceptical of the effectiveness of that money in ameliorating the ills to which it is directed. They are also fascinated by the formulations used to justify why some Australians should give to others. Writing in 1976, Hayek remarked that 'the appeal to "social justice" has … become the most widely used and most effective argument in political discussion. Almost every claim for government action on behalf of particular groups is advanced in its name.'[29]

Progressives, on the other hand, seem to share an egalitarian bent,

---

29 Hayek, 1982, 65.

which generates a strong suspicion that social justice will not rest until all share equally. For this reason, and following earlier attempts to draw lines of absolute poverty (the efforts by Ronald Henderson come to mind), the definition of poverty has become relative.[30] Much of the discussion around a fair division of society's resources seems to stem from the question: what amount of difference is allowed in the deviation from equality? One suggestion is that difference is allowable so long as any changes ensure that the greatest benefit accrues to the least advantaged (the difference principle)[31] or, more expansively, 'the worst off gain as much as they possibly can gain from inequality, so they have no reasonable complaint; and the rest gain even more than the worst off, so they have no reasonable complaint. Thus, all groups gain as much as they can reasonably demand.'[32] The basis for such formulations, however, may be nothing more than a form of insurance against the possibility of bad fortune. They are also under pressure from more radical formulations.

Citizenship theory of the welfare state contends that community membership is the source of the claims citizens have against each other. From community membership flows the welfare rights each can assert and the duties each owes.[33] This concept suggests that all citizens have rights to 'receive what they need to respect their status as full members of society, irrespective of the reasons why they lack resources and opportunity bases.'[34] There is a compensating duty which should exist alongside rights. For example, there is a duty to maintain one's health and to seek gainful employment. By ignoring the reasons why people lack resources and opportunity citizenship rights tends to open the door to significant claims on the resources of others. The concept struggles to answer the question, 'what are rights to welfare rights to?'[35] More fundamentally, it struggles to explain why someone else should do something for you. Despite the balancing duty, there is the distinct possibility of unending claims for example – 'to be compensated for

---

30 Dennis, 1998.
31 John Rawls, *A Theory of Justice*. Harvard University Press, 1971, 54.
32 Brian Barry, *Theories of Justice*. London: Harvest-Wheatsheaf, 1989, 233.
33 Harris, 1987, 145.
34 Harris, 1987, 157.
35 Harris, 1897, 123.

the fact that the society in which I live is not one in which I can be independent.'[36] There is a very large element of blame attaching to unspecified forces; one formulation states that 'If some individuals benefit from a social process which pushes others below the benchmark, compensation is owed.'[37]

The weakness in citizenship theory is that it tries to bypass the legitimation that comes with democratic consent. Social justice delivered by voluntary effort, of which there is a great deal in Australia, needs little or no justification. People should be free to assist others as they see fit. Complications arise, however, when charities acting as agents raise funds from donors to distribute to the poor. In this case, the agent may have their own view of what is socially just; a level of scrutiny of charities is warranted to ensure that donors are well informed of the charities' intentions and performance to ensure that donor intentions are satisfied.[38]

Social justice delivered by government, using taxpayer funds, however, requires consent. Democratic consent provides a solid rationale for government delivering 'social justice'. Politicians seeking permission to raise taxes for the purposes of social justice may make such taxation difficult to criticise, but it does not relieve them of the burden to explain why they should use the taxes so raised to 'care' for others. The situation is even more fraught when politicians have the capacity to buy votes from both givers and receivers. Those who are being taxed often receive considerable benefits, so-called middle-class welfare, which buys their compliance in having money distributed lower down the income scale. Vote buying leads to considerable 'churn', because money is returned to those who paid taxes. One estimate is that about half of welfare transfer payments are pointless churn.[39]

The difference principle, which provides a link between the fortunes of the well-off and poor, and citizenship rights, which assert solidarity as a substitute for charity and insurance, both face the question of whether

---

36 Harris, 1987, 158.
37 Harris, 1987, 163.
38 Gary Johns, 'The Missing Donor.' Submission to the *Scoping Study for national not-for-profit regulator: Consultation Paper.* January 2011.
39 John Humphreys, 'Ending the Churn: A Tax/Welfare Swap.' *Monograph.* Centre for Independent Studies Policy, 2009, 100, 1.

the poor are the architects of their own downfall. As a consequence, others have introduced into the social justice equation the role of personal responsibility – that individuals need to be compensated only for those aspects for which they are not responsible.[40] A major accomplishment of egalitarian theory since John Rawls' work is inclusion of considerations of responsibility. In this way, egalitarian theory has incorporated 'the most appealing idea in the arsenal of the anti-egalitarian Right',[41] that people should be held responsible for their accomplishments. Consideration of personal responsibility, which some call an equal-opportunity approach, corresponds to what most people intuitively believe, that persons should be compensated for certain kinds of bad luck, but should be held responsible for much of what they do. A refinement of the difference principle to incorporate personal responsibility is that policies should maximise the advantage of the worst-off for a given relative effort level (that is, an equality of opportunity policy). Equality of opportunity does not necessarily imply equality of outcomes but; rather, 'level(ling) the playing field so that all have the potential to achieve the same outcomes; whether or not, in the event, they do, depends upon individual choice.'[42]

From a liberal perspective, it is safe to say that welfare rights are, within strict limits, justifiable. A libertarian view, where government provides no protection, would be regarded as too harsh. A liberal view is that some freedom is traded for some protection. Welfare rights would be justified on insurance and charitable grounds, and where there is a very strong presumption towards effort and obligations, and a wary eye on the cost and efficacy of programs. The following formulation is a useful rule of thumb:

1. Welfare rights are not a blank cheque
2. Redistribution that impinges significantly on those obliged to provide is unwarranted
3. Those who can work should work
4. No welfare law should restrict the access of others to employment

---

40 Ronald Dworkin, 'What is Equality? Part 1: Equality of Welfare.' *Philosophy and Public Affairs.* 1981, 10, 185.
41 John E. Roemer, 'Equality of Opportunity: A Progress Report.' *Social Choice and Welfare.* 2002, 19(2), 470.
42 Roemer, 2002, 456.

or opportunities to profit

5. No welfare law should create 'an army of bureaucrats' whose livelihood rests on perpetuation of generations of welfare dependency, and

6. 'Welfare rights do not supplant private charity'.[43]

Loren Lomasky's formulation provides a practical and worldly introduction to the limits of social justice in a liberal democracy. But the ultimate arbiters of fairness are Australian voters. Redistributive justice in Australia most likely reflects the values of Australians.

Advance Australia fair

It is important, therefore, to know what Australians actually think is a fair distribution of resources. Following Saunders' discussion, it appears that Australians recognise three broad concepts of fairness – egalitarian, meritocratic, and liberal.[44] The egalitarian definition of fairness focuses on the final distribution of resources. Anything that flattens the distribution of income and wealth is fair; anything that makes it less equal is unfair.

A meritocratic definition of fairness hinges on the principle of 'just deserts'. Unequal outcomes are fair provided everybody has had a chance to compete on an equal basis. In particular, fairness requires that the most hard-working and talented people should reap the highest rewards (the meritocratic approach of 'ability plus effort'). This will only happen if there are no major obstacles blocking the achievement of meritorious individuals from the least advantaged backgrounds (the equality of opportunity approach).

In contrast, the classical liberal conception of fairness denies the relevance of any distributional principle, whether egalitarian or meritocratic. Fairness requires an open system governed by the rule of law. It is judged by procedures, not outcomes. People must be free to accumulate assets and to transfer them as they see fit. Provided these rules are followed, the result is 'fair'.

The three principles of fairness are logically incompatible. It cannot

---

43 Loren Lomasky, 'Justice to Charity.' In Alan F Frankel et al (editors), *The Just Society.* Cambridge University Press, 1995, 48.
44 Peter Saunders, 'What is "Fair" About a Fair Go?' *Policy.* Centre for Independent Studies, 2004, volume 20(1).

be simultaneously fair to have a steeply progressive tax regime and to reward people for hard work, or allow people to keep what they have gained through voluntary exchange. Nevertheless, because there are competing concepts of fairness and a continuing debate about which concept should dominate, the actual outcome is an amalgamation.

A 2003 survey of public opinion in Australia measured public support for each of the three definitions of fairness. Table 2 shows that 85 percent supported a meritocratic definition of fairness as reward for talent and effort; 60 percent supported a classical liberal definition of fairness as outcomes from voluntary transactions; and 33 percent supported an egalitarian definition of fairness emphasising the reduction of income inequality.[45]

Table 2. Australian support for three definitions of fairness

Percent of population agreeing with:	
Meritocratic: 'In a fair society, people's incomes should depend on how hard they work and how talented they are'.	85
Classical liberal: In a fair society, people's incomes should depend on how much other people value the services they provide'.	60
Egalitarian: 'In a fair society, nobody should get an income a lot bigger or a lot smaller than anybody else gets'.	33
Options:	
Liberal + meritocracy	36
All three	19
Meritocracy + egalitarian	7
Egalitarianism only	5
Does not agree with any	5
Liberal + egalitarian	3
Classical liberal only	2

Source: Peter Saunders, 'What is "Fair" About a Fair Go?' *Policy*. Centre for Independent Studies, 2004, volume 20(1), 8.

Australians support greater equality of income and wealth distribution, but when an egalitarian option is put together with the

---

45 As reported in Saunders, 2004, 8.

competing meritocratic and classical liberal options, the support drops dramatically. For those who equate popular support for fairness with egalitarianism at the heart of social justice, the minority who support an egalitarian definition nearly always combine it with support for one or both of the other two conceptions of fairness (even though these are logically incompatible with egalitarianism). Only one in 20 Australians thinks fairness is solely to do with achieving more equal outcomes.

A recent study in the United Kingdom tested similar ideas of what might constitute a fair society. The study compared a 'free market' conception (fairness based on what the market is prepared to pay), a meritocratic one (based on getting rewards for effort and ability), and an egalitarian one (based on equal rewards regardless of effort or ability). Another question asked respondents to choose between equality of opportunity and egalitarianism.

Results were very similar to Australia and indicated that a majority of people thought that fairness was mainly a question of people getting what they deserved, rather than being about equal treatment. Table 3 shows this was true of voters of all political persuasions, where 63 percent of people say that 'fairness is about getting what you deserve' and 26 percent say that 'fairness is about equality'. In other words, people's idea of fairness is strongly reciprocal – something for something.

Table 3. UK support for three definitions of fairness

Percent of the population agreeing with:	
Meritocratic: In a fair society, people's incomes should depend on how hard they work and how talented they are	85
Classical liberal: In a fair society, people's incomes should depend on how much other people value the services they provide	63
Egalitarian: In a fair society, nobody should get an income a lot bigger or a lot smaller than anybody else gets	41
Equality of opportunity: You can have a fair society even if people's incomes are quite unequal, as long as you have equality of opportunity	73

Source: Neil O'Brien, 'Just Deserts? Attitudes to Fairness, Poverty and Welfare Reform.' *Research Note*. Policy Exchange, April 2011, 9.

The meritocratic conception was most popular, with support fairly similar among different social groups, and supporters of different parties. Support was somewhat stronger among more highly educated voters, higher social classes and broadsheet readers. The free market conception was less popular, but again had similar levels of support among different groups. Interestingly, Labour voters agreed with the statement, and Liberal Democratic voters were the most strongly in favour of all. The egalitarian conception was less popular, and the most divisive. Labour voters, Liberal Democrats and lower social classes agreed with the statement on balance, while Conservatives, graduates, and higher social groups strongly disagreed.[46]

Social justice, to the extent that it is an egalitarian philosophy, is not well supported in the electorate. Moreover, it is not regarded as particularly fair. Nevertheless, more out of charity and insurance than feelings of solidarity, citizens understand the need for assistance to the poor. They may perceive a link between the fortunes of the well off and the poor, but not one where the rich gained their wealth at the expense of the poor. The emerging elements in the debate are concentration on individual choice and effort as the limiting factors on delivery of social justice. This is an uncomfortable field for social justice advocates, who, in designing systems of redistribution, prefer never to blame anyone other than the rich for poverty.

---

46 Neil O'Brien, 'Just Deserts? Attitudes to Fairness, Poverty and Welfare Reform.' *Research Note*. Policy Exchange, April 2011, 9.

2
The welfare state grows and grows

Julie Novak

> *One writer ... decried the emergence of a 'stratified' Australian society as a result of a flattening income tax structure and labour market deregulation, both seen to be violations of previously hardwon social justice gains.*[1]
>
> - An Australian Fabian

Crisis, what crisis?

Numerous protagonists favouring extension of the Australian welfare state have often done so historically with affirming nods to the concept of 'social justice,' a key element of which rests on a program of achieving equality of outcomes among individuals of varying talents and capabilities.

While the social justice lexicon has somewhat withered as a means of framing discourse within Commonwealth and state parliaments, partly deriving from general recognition of the importance of economic growth in lifting material living standards for all regardless of prior income or wealth, the term maintains particular resonance within the Socialist Left faction of Labor, and the Greens, as well as for certain charities and other nongovernment organisations. The Australian Fabians, a think tank with enduring links with the Labor Party, have long been at the forefront of defending the role of government in welfare on social justice grounds, and to extend this role wherever possible.

The policy platform of the Australian Greens at the 2010 federal election included a range of policies, effectively ratcheting up the size and scope of the welfare state, to ensure a goal of 'income equity

---

1 T. Evans, 'Policies for the Future: Welfare State is in Crisis.' Australian Fabians (undated).

and social justice.'[2] The president of the St Vincent de Paul Society's National Social Justice Committee, Terry McCarthy, speaking in 2005, portrayed social justice as nothing less than 'a Christian obligation.'[3] He saw enlistment of collective actions by all levels of government, through cash transfers and delivery of services, as the most effective way to secure greater equality consistent with the social justice obligation.

Belief in the concept of social justice subscribed to by the political Left is intellectually suspect because, according to Friedrich Hayek, it represents the coupling of the 'weasel' word of 'social' with an erroneous interpretation of the word 'justice.' As fundamental an intellectual error that social justice is, a policy conviction that social justice provides the intellectual framework to correct variations in income or wealth, in every instance where such tendencies are found, radically lowers the threshold by which coercive state interventions may be justified to strive for an *ex-ante* desired result.

Such tendencies have been observed with regard to development of the welfare state in Australia, rationalised by many of its proponents as an important basis upon which to achieve social justice objectives.

What is the welfare state?

There remains much controversy within academic writings concerning a commonly accepted definition of the 'welfare state'. Asa Briggs devised a definition in the early 1960s that is now commonly cited in sociology textbooks:

> [a] welfare state is a state in which organized power is deliberately used … in an effort to modify the play of market forces in at least three directions … by guaranteeing individuals and families a minimum income irrespective of the market value of their work or their property; … by narrowing the extent of insecurity by enabling individuals and families to meet certain 'social contingencies' … which lead otherwise to individual and family crises; and, … by ensuring that all citizens without distinction of status or class are offered the best standards available in relation to a certain agreed

2 Australian Greens, 'Social Services Policy.' 2008.
3 T. McCarthy, 'The Pursuit of Social Justice in Australia: a Difficult Task with the Threat from Within.' National Social Justice Committee, St Vincent de Paul Society, 2005.

range of social services.[4]

Notwithstanding Briggs' effort, an important reason why there remains a lack of definitional agreement is that the nature of the welfare state can vary considerably from country to country. For this reason, Esping-Anderson distinguishes between 'liberal,' 'conservative' and 'social-democratic' welfare states based on the degree to which individuals can receive welfare as a 'right' and, hence, not rely on markets, the degree of redistribution, and level of universality achieved by a welfare system.[5]

The Anglo-Saxon economies of the United Kingdom and United States largely satisfy the liberal welfare state notion, according great weight to individuality and private economic action and which provide relatively parsimonious levels of state welfare. The implicit objective of the liberal welfare state, with its means-tested benefits and modest social insurance plans, is to encourage workforce participation and minimisation of taxpayer exposure to welfare dependency.

Esping-Anderson uses the conservative welfare regime to describe the models maintained by continental European states such as France, Germany and Italy. This type of welfare state attempts to maintain traditional family structures by discouraging women from participating in the labour market. The state is prepared to replace the market in order to provide payments and services, but does so only once a family's means of economic self-reliance is exhausted.

The third strand of Esping-Anderson's welfare capitalism is the social-democratic welfare state. It is commonly associated with Scandinavian countries. There is a high degree of universalism in provision of welfare services, in which women are encouraged to work and receive social services such as subsidised childcare. Others can disengage with the market and access welfare benefits if they so wish. According to Esping-Anderson, '[a]ll benefit; all are dependent; and all will presumably feel obliged to pay.'[6]

Several scholars have critically appraised Esping-Anderson's

---

4 A. Briggs, 'The Welfare State in Historical Perspective.' In C. Pierson and F. G. Castles (editors) *The Welfare State Reader.* 2nd edition, Cambridge: Polity Press, 2006, 16.
5 G. Esping-Anderson, *The Three Worlds of Welfare Capitalism.* Cambridge: Polity Press, 1990.
6 Esping-Anderson, 1990, 28.

suggestion that there exist only three models of governmental welfare within the OECD. Castles has suggested that the welfare states of Australia and New Zealand must be distinguished from the rest because of what he described as the 'wage earners' welfare state' prevalent in the Antipodes. The traditional, centralised method of wages determination through industrial tribunals intended to accord labourers a 'living wage' were designed to ensure that workers need not rely on welfare payments and social services in order to sustain themselves and their families.

Another reason why welfare states tend to defy definition is that size and scope can change, sometimes dramatically, over time.

Underlying the observed trend of secular growth in the Australian welfare state has been an extension in the purpose of welfare from that of providing a limited array of payments and services to those who cannot participate in the market economy on their own accord, to a much broader system with greater reach throughout the population, preoccupied with countering multiple conceptions of 'social need' that may have little to do with remediation of absolute poverty.

That the welfare state can be subject to change leads to an appreciation of the idea that its evolution is shaped by complex and country-specific historical, legal and political developments, as well as economic and social forces.

The conception of the Australian welfare state adopted in this chapter is greater in scope than that of redistributive cash payments to individuals only, though the coverage is more refined than that implied by Castles' broad conception.

This chapter takes an intermediate position to conceive of the welfare state as comprised of social security direct cash grants to individuals and families and government grants to voluntary agencies, as well as non-marketable government expenditures in education and health care.[7]

By adopting this coverage, this chapter describes the development of a welfare state intended to meet the social needs of individuals throughout their lives, from the cradle to the grave.

---

7 Reliance on this coverage understates the total size of the Australian welfare state, as it excludes a range of government payments and services, for example public housing provision, government housing assistance for those on low incomes, and subsidies for aged care.

The long evolution of the Australian welfare state

From relatively modest beginnings, at least from the perspective of what exists today, the Australian welfare state now consumes a substantial proportion of government budgets. Commonwealth and state government expenditure on the welfare state has risen, in nominal terms, from $8.3 million in 1901-02 to $308.3 billion in 2009-10. Since 1973-74, the first full fiscal year of the Whitlam Labor Government, welfare state spending has grown by an astronomical 4,838 percent. Commonwealth expenditure accounts for almost two-thirds of that increase.

Figure 1 illustrates the growth in the welfare state from the turn of the 20th century, expressed in terms of government expenditure as a share of gross domestic product (GDP).

Figure 1. Welfare state expenditure as a percentage of GDP

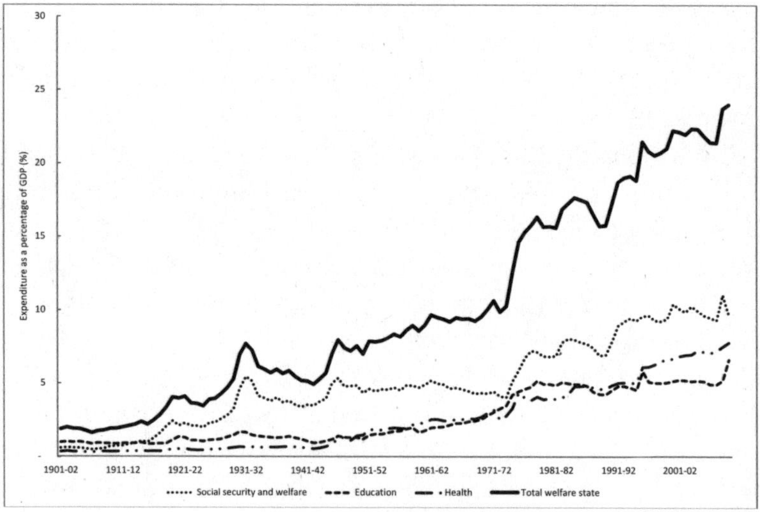

Expressed in current prices. Includes Commonwealth and state expenditure on selective social security benefits, education, and health care.

Source: ABS, Australian System of National Accounts, 200910, cat. no. 5204.0, 2010; ABS, Government Finance Statistics, Australia, 200910, cat. no. 5512.0, 2010; R. Mendelsohn, The Condition of The People: Social Welfare in Australia 19001975. Sydney: George Allen & Unwin, 1979; R. A. Foster, Australian Economic Statistics 194950 to 1994-95, Sydney: Reserve Bank of Australia, 1996; W. Vamplew (ed), Australians, Historical Statistics, Fairfax, Syme & Weldon Associates, Broadway, 1987.

In 1901-02 total welfare spending was equivalent to two percent of GDP, the states of New South Wales and Victoria having introduced a means tested age pension in 1900. During the first decade of federation the states also maintained secular government education for children and, in limited instances, provided grant payments to not-for-profit hospitals run mainly by religious orders.

Despite incursions into the social security sphere by the Commonwealth during the next decade, including a national age pension in 1908, an invalid pension (later renamed disability support pension) in 1910 and a maternity allowance in 1912, the overall share of welfare state spending to GDP remained reasonably stable during the first two decades of the Australian federation.

During the 1920s some important developments in welfare state policy transpired. These included an unemployment insurance scheme introduced by the Theodore Labor Government in Queensland in 1923 and a child endowment scheme by the Lang Labor Government in New South Wales in 1927. The larger states also reorganised the structure of publicly provided school education services to promote educational participation.

The Nationalist Prime Minister, S. M. Bruce, in part spurred on by criticisms by the Labor Party that the Commonwealth had lost momentum to build upon previous welfare state 'reforms,' investigated the feasibility of a compulsory national insurance scheme to provide sickness, invalidity, maternity and superannuation benefits to all insured members and their families, as well as limited payments for children of members unable to work.[8]

Introduction of legislation in the Commonwealth parliament in 1928 to put a scheme into effect brought fierce opposition from business groups and fraternal societies who feared rising costs of employment and a loss in memberships respectively. Events the following year led to a change of government. The controversial proposal lapsed. A similar fate met a later attempt to introduce a national insurance scheme by the Lyons Coalition government in 1938.

One of the key strategies adopted in response to the Great Depression

---

8 B. U. Ratchford, *Public Expenditures in Australia*. Durham, NC: Duke University Press, 1959.

of the early 1930s was a comprehensive program of expenditure reductions, enabling Commonwealth and state governments to restore budget balance. The Premiers' Plan of mid-1931 incorporated reductions to Commonwealth age and invalid pensions and maternity allowances, and other payments, which were duly implemented.

The rising number of unemployed people led governments to provide special relief to affected families as well as embark on capital works to employ unemployed workers, financed in some cases by special taxes on wages and salaries. It is estimated that as many as 673,800 families nationally received some form of relief during the Depression.[9] As a result of the Great Depression, welfare state expenditures, both at Commonwealth and state levels, increased to about eight percent of GDP.

The period during World War II was exemplified by significant changes to the Australian welfare state by the Commonwealth, to the extent that 'Australia entered World War II with only a fragmentary welfare provision; by the end of the war it had constructed a "welfare state".'[10]

The Menzies United Australia Party-Country Party Coalition government introduced a Commonwealth child endowment scheme in 1941, financed by a payroll tax, which superseded a NSW scheme established in 1927. This was followed by Commonwealth widows' pensions (1942), funeral benefits for invalid and oldage pensioners (1943), and sickness and unemployment benefits (1944) introduced by the Curtin Labor Government. The constitutionality of these payments was ensured in 1946 by a successful referendum. Extended benefits under existing schemes were also provided, including provision of an allowance to the wife of an invalid pensioner, and to her first child below sixteen years of age, while rates for age and invalid pensions and maternity allowances were increased.[11]

In 1943 the Curtin Labor Government, adopting a recommendation

---

9 C. M. White, *Mastering Risk: Environment, Markets and Politics in Australian Economic History*. South Melbourne: Oxford University Press, 1992.
10 A. Herscovitch and D. Stanton 'History of Social Security in Australia.' *Family Matters*. 2008, 80, 54.
11 T. H. Kewley, 'The Development of the Social Services' in C. H. Grattan (editor), *Australia*. Berkeley: University of California Press, 1947; Ratchford, 1959.

of a high-powered Parliamentary Committee on Social Security, established a trust account called the National Welfare Fund from which welfare payments were to be financed. The Minister for Post War Reconstruction, Ben Chifley, noted 'the great advantage of the scheme is that the fund accumulates surpluses in good times and distributes purchasing power widely at times when business conditions flag or falter.'[12]

In contrast to previous attempts to establish a contributory insurance fund, the National Welfare Fund was entirely financed from consolidated revenue of an amount equal to £30 million or one-fourth of the proceeds from the income tax on individuals, whichever was less.[13]

Initially only a selective range of welfare payments were financed by the Fund, but by 1946 all social services were to be financed from Fund reserves. A special graduated tax on incomes, called the 'Social Service Contribution', was the main source of revenue for the Fund, in addition to the payroll tax on employers.

Upon gaining office in 1949, the Menzies Liberal-Country Party Government amended the legislation governing the National Welfare Fund that incorporated the Social Service Contribution into general income tax assessments and pooled funds into consolidated revenue. In effect, the contribution was treated as part of general revenue. The Hawke Labor Government eventually abolished the trust fund underpinning this scheme in 1985.

For much of its period in office from 1949 to 1972, and contrary to perceptions by social justice advocates that they harboured a niggardly attitude towards welfare, the Coalition governments of the Commonwealth raised rates for many payments, such as age and invalid pensions, on a regular basis, typically in excess of the cost of living.[14] For example, in 1961-62, the Government substantially increased certain benefits, including sickness and unemployment payments and age, invalid and widows' pensions. At the time the changes in 1961-62

12 B. Chifley, 'Planning for Peace III: Social Security Scheme: National Insurance Rejected', *The Sydney Morning Herald*, December 3 1943, 4.
13 Kewley, 1947.
14 N. G. Butlin, A. Barnard and J. J. Pincus, *Government and Capitalism: Public and Private Choice in Twentieth Century Australia*. London: George Allen & Unwin, 1982.

were the largest experienced during the decade 1954-55 to 1964-65.[15]

Meanwhile, the Menzies Government effectively doubled those eligible for the child endowment by providing a weekly payment of five shillings for the first child in each family from 1950. In 1964, the Commonwealth extended the child endowment to student children aged between 16 and 21.

From the 1950s a host of new benefits including free medical and hospital treatment for pensioners (1951), supplementary assistance for pensioners paying private rents (1958), and a higher rate of pension for single pensioners (1963) were introduced. There was also a major liberalisation of the means testing provisions on pensions, including the exclusion of income from property in 1954 and a doubling of the income and property limits at which pension eligibility ceased in 1969.[16]

During the 1950s and 1960s both Commonwealth and state governments undertook additional expenditures in school and tertiary education in efforts to increase student enrolments substantially. This reflected a range of factors, including demographic change in the form of the 'baby boom,' structural change in the economy with an increasing emphasis upon skills attainment, greater community demands for human capital investment and, during the 1960s, cost pressures leading to increasing government subsidisation of Catholic and independent schools.

During the 23 years of federal Coalition government, 1949-1972, the relative size of the Australian welfare state at Commonwealth and state levels increased from eight percent of GDP in 1949-50 to 11 percent in 1971-72. In sharp contrast, the following three years under the Whitlam Labor government were associated with a sharp spike in welfare state expenditure to 15 percent of GDP by 1975-76.

Significant policy changes undertaken by Labor included gradual abolition of the means test on age pensions, initially for people aged 75 and over (in 1973) and between 70 and 74 years (1975). This represented the Whitlam Government's policy favouring a universal age pensions system.

15 M. Artis and R. Wallace, 'Assessing the Fiscal Impact', in N. Runcie (editor) *Australian Monetary and Fiscal Policy: Selected Readings*, volume 1, London: University of London Press, 1971.
16 T. H. Kewley, *Social Security in Australia: 190072*. Sydney: Sydney University Press, 1973; Butlin, Barnard and Pincus, 1982.

Other new forms of welfare payments were also introduced during this period. From December 1974 a Handicapped Child's Allowance of $10 for parents or guardians caring for severely disabled children at home was introduced, while a pension-style payment was enacted in 1975 for single parents not receiving a widow's pension.[17]

Another major innovation during the Whitlam era was the introduction of Medibank universal health insurance system in July 1975. Replacing the system of voluntary health insurance, Medibank entailed free treatment for public patients in public hospitals and subsidies to private hospitals enabling them to reduce their fees. Under an arrangement with the states, the Commonwealth extended grants to public hospitals equal to 50 percent of their net operating running costs.[18]

The Commonwealth also assumed responsibility to finance fully the tertiary education system from the states, abolishing university fees for undergraduates.

Of the significance of these developments, a former Treasury Secretary, Ken Henry, observed three and a half decades later that 'the total increase in [Commonwealth] government expenditure under the Whitlam government is fully explained by an expansion of the social policy role of government in health, education and social security and welfare.'[19]

Compared with the Whitlam experience, the trend in welfare state expenditure under the Fraser Government was an exercise in self-restraint, rising during that period by only two percent of GDP, even if social security spending commitments rose as a consequence of additional unemployment benefit recipients during the severe 1981-82 recession.

Under the Hawke and Keating Labor governments, Commonwealth and state expenditures on social security, education and health care increased from 17 percent of GDP in 1983-84 to 19 percent in 1994-95. As explained below, as much as these governments undertook

---

17 Herscovitch and Stanton, 2008.
18 A. Biggs, 'Medicare.' *Background Brief*. Australian Parliamentary Library, 2004.
19 K. Henry, 'Fiscal Policy: More Than Just a National Budget', *Address to the Whitlam Institute*. 2009, 13.

explicit policy decisions to extend the welfare state, its growth was also influenced by a severe recession during the early 1990s, which left more than one million Australians out of work, and the subsequent jobless recovery.

The Commonwealth invasion of the states' field of constitutional responsibility of health significantly increased in February 1984 with the introduction of the Medicare program. This scheme of universal, tax-financed health insurance provides public hospital services to patients free at the point of entry, whilst providing generous rebates on consultation and treatment costs for general practitioner and medical specialist services.

While rationalised by the Hawke Government as an initiative to promote social equity, Medicare has had a range of adverse consequences. These have included diminution of private health insurance membership (at least, until corrective, yet fiscally burdensome, policy actions were introduced from 1996), quantity restrictions by the states including bed rationalisation and treatment waiting lists, lax cost controls and, with a projected increase in population ageing, significant risks of increasing tax costs in the future.

In 1992, the Keating Government introduced a compulsory superannuation guarantee, legally obligating employers to pay an amount based on employee wages (currently nine per cent) into a superannuation fund.

While this scheme has been predicated on the basis of reducing reliance upon age pension payments in the longer term, it has likely contributed to a reduction in private savings and has deprived working-age people of alternative uses of funds compulsorily diverted into superannuation.

Under the Howard Government expenditure on the welfare state also increased, to 21 per cent of GDP by 2006-07. In similar fashion to previous governments, the Howard Government frequently increased benefit rates of welfare payments such as aged pensions and carer allowances for favoured constituencies.

Recognising the perverse fiscal dynamics of passive welfare, the Howard Government also promoted welfare reform to improve participation of recipients in economic activity, such as those receiving unemployment benefit, disability support pension, and sole parent payments, by reinforcing a sense of 'mutual obligation' between recipients and taxpayers.

A development of significance for the Australian welfare state transpired in 2000, with a generalised increase in rate benefits in an attempt to shield those on lower incomes from the price effects of the goods and services tax. This has served as an important precedent for governments to use the welfare state apparatus to compensate individuals and families for changes in relative prices.

A new regime of Family Tax Benefits was introduced in the same year to assist families with the cost of raising children more effectively, while the Commonwealth enacted a new regime of funding non-government schools in 2001 to empower parental choices in schooling.

For their part, the states undertook additional measures to promote the attainment of secondary schooling qualifications or vocational training by young people in the form of so-called 'learn or earn' funding guarantees.

Welfare spending has ratcheted upwards again under the Rudd and Gillard Labor governments. This partly derived from increases in unemployment benefits during the 'global financial crisis' (GFC). By and large the government has maintained, at least in rhetoric, commitments to promote the capacity of welfare recipients to attain meaningful work, reducing the exposure of taxpayers to the future growth of the welfare state.

Over the past year the Commonwealth has outlined welfare payment rate increases as compensation for cascading price changes under a proposed carbon tax. There has also been preliminary work undertaken with the states on a national insurance scheme for people with disabilities to replace state government and voluntary sector management.

The observed long run increase in welfare state expenditure not only reflects explicit government policy decisions but changes in the number of welfare and social services recipients (Figure 2). In 2009-10, about 22 percent of Australians, and almost one in three of working age, received a form of social security payment from the Commonwealth. This degree of dependency is very high considering the background of generalised economic growth and sustained improvements in material wellbeing, including growth in the variety of products available to the general public and real price reductions for most conveniences of life.[20]

Figure 2. Recipients of social security payments for individuals

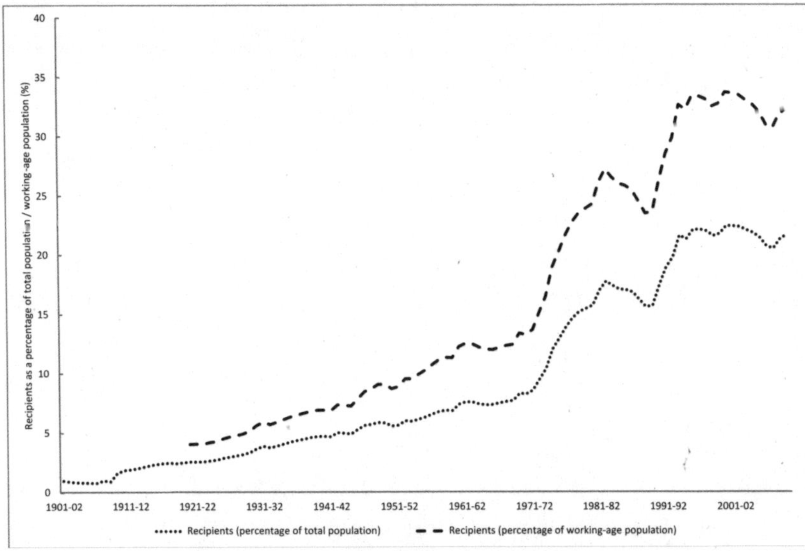

Expressed as a share of total Australian population or working-age population. Includes recipients of Age Pension, Invalid Pension/Disability Support Pension, Wife Pension, unemployment benefits, sickness benefits, Special Benefit, special circumstances benefits, sole parent and widow payments, partnered parent payments, carer payments, and rehabilitation or mobility allowances.

Source: ABS, Australian Demographic Statistics, December 2010, cat. no. 3101.0; ABS, Australian Historical Population Statistics, cat. no. 3105.0.65.001; D. Daniels, 'Social security payments for the aged, people with disabilities and carers 1901 to 2010', Parliamentary Library, 2011; D. Daniels 'Social security payments for people caring for children, 1912 to 2006', Parliamentary Library, 2006; D. Daniels, 'Social security payments for the unemployed, the sick and those in special circumstances, 1942 to 2006.' Parliamentary Library, 2006; Department of Families, Housing, Community Services and Indigenous Affairs, 'Income Support Customers: A Statistical Overview 2010.' Statistical Paper No. 9, 2010; W. Vamplew (ed), Australians, Historical Statistics, Fairfax, Syme & Weldon Associates, Broadway, 1987.

---

20 For an analysis of the consequences of these trends for the measurement of inequality, see W. Wilkinson, 'Thinking Clearly About Income Inequality.' *Policy Analysis*. No. 640. Cato Institute, 2009.

As noted by Saunders, important drivers of rising welfare dependency have been unemployment benefits and disability support pensions paid to people (mainly men) without jobs, as well as the increase in parenting payments to single parents (mainly women) living in a household without a 'breadwinner' engaged in employment (Figure 3).[21]

Figure 3. Recipients of disability support pensions, unemployment benefits and payments for sole parents and widows

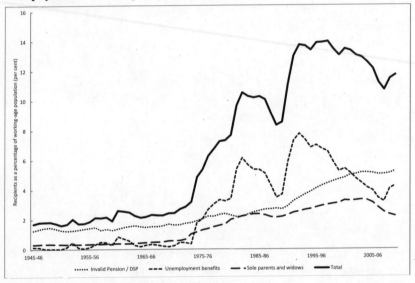

Expressed as a share of working-age population.

Source: ABS, *Australian Demographic Statistics,* December 2010, cat. no. 3101.0; ABS, *Australian Historical Population Statistics,* cat. no. 3105.0.65.001; D. Daniels, 'Social security payments for the aged, people with disabilities and carers 1901 to 2010', Parliamentary Library, 2011; D. Daniels, 'Social security payments for the unemployed, the sick and those in special circumstances, 1942 to 2006', Parliamentary Library, 2006; Department of Families, Housing, Community Services and Indigenous Affairs, 'Income Support Customers: A Statistical Overview 2010', Statistical Paper No. 9, 2010; W. Vamplew (editor), *Australians, Historical Statistics,* Fairfax, Syme & Weldon Associates, Broadway, 1987.

Another important element of the overall growth in the welfare state has been the growth of Commonwealth payments to assist

21 P. Saunders, *Australia's Welfare Habit and How to Kick It.* Sydney: Duffy & Snellgrove, 2004.

families with the costs of raising their children.[22] The national child endowment scheme, introduced by the Menzies United Australia Party Government, provided assistance to about 487,700 eligible families (with about 909,900 children) in 1941-42.[23] Under the existing regime of Family Tax Benefits, about 2.1 million eligible families (with about five million children) received some form of payment in 2007-08.[24]

The Family Tax Benefit and other payment regimes have been criticised within academic and policy circles as reflecting part of a broader trend extending welfare to middle and upper class individuals and families who can afford to look after their own needs.

The increasing trend of taxpayers to pay taxes, only to have these returned (less administrative costs) as welfare benefits, has been labelled 'fiscal churn.' It has recently been estimated that, in effect, 42 percent of Australian households pay no net income tax as a consequence of this churning effect.[25] Such wasteful practices suggest that the well-targeted approach of the means tested Australian welfare state has been increasingly compromised with the passage of time.

Conclusion

The role of government in providing welfare payments and social services has been radically extended since their inception. This growing involvement has come at the great cost of crowding out viable non-government means of meeting welfare needs. And, as Green and Cromwell show in an important historical profile of Australian welfare, it is entirely inaccurate to depict the period prior to the twentieth century government welfare state as a 'fend for oneself' environment of no welfare.[26]

This is because a complex ecology of arrangements, such as

---

22 This includes families benefiting as a consequence of the subsidisation of education services and child care, which are excluded from the discussion that follows.
23 D. Daniels, 'Social Security Payments for People Caring for Children: 1912 to 2008.' *Australian Parliamentary Library*, 2009.
24 Department of Families, Housing, Community Services and Indigenous Affairs, *Annual Report 2009-10*. Commonwealth of Australia, Canberra, 2010.
25 G. Megalogenis, 'The TaxFree Middle Class.' *The Australian*. September 20 2008.
26 D. G. Green and L. G. Cromwell, *Mutual Aid or Welfare State: Australia's Friendly Societies*. Sydney: George Allen & Unwin, 1984.

voluntary mutual-aid associations, not-for-profit hospitals and health care services, and schools established by religious orders, provided benefits and services to a substantial, and growing, proportion of the population. The growth of the welfare state, with public sector involvement as its organising principle, has destroyed this essential component of the broader fabric of Australian civil society.

A plethora of government cash benefits for individuals and families and services have built up over time, complementing a wide range of services either directly provided or subsidised by governments, in particular, in education and health. While the Australian Labor Party and, more recently, the Greens have been active sponsors of an expanded welfare state on various grounds, including promotion of 'social justice' objectives, liberal-conservative governments have also played a conspicuous role in growth of the Australian welfare state.

The growth of the welfare state has continued in spite of the generalised improvement in living standards enjoyed by most Australians, which should in itself enable them to cope more effectively with the vicissitudes of life.

Alarmingly, the growing welfare state has not only led to a substantial rise in the numbers of people dependent upon the state for their comforts or livelihoods, but to the displacement of civil society and long-cherished values of self-reliance and individual responsibility.

Even for the most forceful advocates of 'social justice,' these features of the Australian welfare state should surely give cause for great concern.

3
Are Equal Societies Better Societies?

Peter Saunders

If we understood our social needs and susceptibilities we would see that a less unequal society causes dramatically lower rates of ill-health and social problems because it provides us with a better-fitting shoe.[1]

In 2009, Richard Wilkinson and Kate Pickett published *The Spirit Level: Why Equality is Better for Everyone*. They claimed that more equal societies perform better on almost every social and psychological indicator than those which are less equal. Using a series of graphs, the authors showed people in more equal countries appear to live longer, fewer of them are murdered, literacy and numeracy rates are higher, mental illness is lower, trust is stronger, fewer people are locked up in prison, bullying is less common, obesity is less of a problem, and so on. Reinforcing these findings, they also showed that in the USA, the states with the greatest income inequality typically have the worst social and psychological outcomes.

On the basis of all this evidence, Wilkinson and Pickett audaciously claimed that almost everyone would benefit if incomes were made more equal. According to them, it is not just the poor whose lives could be improved by more equal shares; the rich would gain too. This is

---

1 Richard Wilkinson and Kate Pickett, *The Spirit Level: Why Equality is Better for Everyone*. Penguin, 2nd edition, 2010, 213.

because human beings evolved to share. For thousands of years, while living in small hunter-gatherer bands, we shared food. But in modern capitalist societies, we are expected to be competitive, individualistic and acquisitive. The result is that we all become miserable, aggressive and sick; those at the bottom of the heap suffer worst of all.

Much of this argument is familiar from Marx's writings in the nineteenth century. Marx also believed that capitalism warps human nature and leads to widespread alienation of human beings from one another, and from their essential nature. The reason *The Spirit Level* has attracted so much attention, however, is that Wilkinson and Pickett pack their book full of graphs and statistics which seem to back up what they are saying with the power of scientific evidence. Their book seems to pull the rug from under the feet of small-state conservatives and laissez-faire liberals, for how could anyone oppose radical income redistribution when it can be shown, with scientific evidence, that it increases *everybody's* happiness?

The Spirit Level has reinvigorated the Left by investing its traditional beliefs with an aura of science. A former deputy leader of the British Labour Party says it 'demonstrates the scientific truth of the assertion that social democrats have made for a hundred years ... that all of us have much to gain from the creation of a more equal society.'[2] And, in Australia, Wilkinson's 'evidence' has been cited to support the argument that the ALP should return to a radical, egalitarian agenda, at the heart of social justice which will promote 'citizenship and community'.[3]

But when we scrutinise Wilkinson and Pickett's evidence, it becomes clear that this is a book built on the flimsiest foundations. There are many problems with their analysis, but five are crucial: selection bias; choice of indicators; their use of evidence; spurious causation; and the neglect of alternative explanations. It is a matter of some concern that a book so flawed should still be attracting the rapt attention of so many academics and policy-makers.

---

2 Roy Hattersley, 'Last among equals' *New Statesman*. March 16 2009.
3 Tim Soutphommasane claims 'A Growing Number of Scholars Agree More Equal Societies Enjoy Higher Levels of Happiness and Social Cohesion.' *The Australian*. August 25 2010.

Selection bias

Wilkinson and Pickett accept that in poor countries, capitalist development can raise well-being across the board, even while increasing income inequalities. But beyond a certain point, what matters for human happiness, they say, is not more affluence, but more equal distribution.

With this in mind, they set out to analyse the link between income distribution and well-being in the fifty wealthiest nations in the world. In their book, however, they include only twenty-three of them. This is partly because they excluded countries with a population less than three million, on the grounds that they did not want to include tiny tax havens. But their three million population threshold was unnecessarily restrictive, for countries in the top 50 like Slovenia, Trinidad & Tobago, Estonia, Latvia, Gabon and Botswana all have populations below three million, but none could be described as tax havens.

They also say they dropped any country where the statistics they needed were not available. This seems to have excluded another 21 cases. But in all but two of these the data are readily available. In *When Prophecy Fails*, I have successfully included them in replicated analyses.[4] A lot of countries missing from *The Spirit Level* were therefore left out for no good reason.

Wilkinson and Pickett deny this. They still maintain against their critics that in drawing their sample of countries, they 'applied a strict set of criteria ... with no departures or exceptions.'[5] But this is clearly untrue. Where, for example, is South Korea? With a population of 48 million, it is certainly large enough to have been included. Its GDP per head is greater than Portugal's, so it also obviously passes Wilkinson and Pickett's richness test, for they include Portugal in their sample. And there is no shortage of relevant statistics on the country, as is demonstrated by the fact that I managed to include it in almost every graph in *When Prophecy Fails*.

Would the 27 countries they omitted have confirmed the patterns they found for the 23 countries they included? The answer is they would not.

---

4 Peter Saunders, *When Prophecy Fails*. Sydney: Centre for Independent Studies, 2011 (first edition published as *Beware False Prophets*, London: Policy Exchange 2010). I draw extensively on this book in what follows.
5 Wilkinson, 2010, 280.

Wilkinson and Pickett ended up with a sample heavily skewed towards western Europe (16 of their 23 countries), and heavily biased against eastern Europe (11 cases omitted). Slovenia, Hungary and the Czech Republic, for example, are all left out, even though they are richer countries than Portugal, which is retained. Omissions like these have had a critical impact on their results. Many of the countries that were dropped have relatively equal income distributions but perform badly on their various indicators of well-being. Conversely, some, like Hong Kong and South Korea, are relatively unequal in income distribution, but tend to score well on the wellbeing indicators. What Wilkinson and Pickett have done is to engineer a selective sample which is most amenable to the thesis they want to 'prove.'

Choice of indicators

The key proposition in *The Spirit Level* is that people are happier, and societies more cohesive, when income differences are narrower. But how are we to measure personal well-being and social cohesiveness? Some measures show things are worse in more unequal countries, but others suggest they are better. Wilkinson and Pickett always seem to pick the former, never the latter, and they offer no clear rationale for the choices they make.[6]

For example, they show that drug abuse appears to be more widespread in more unequal countries, but they say nothing about alcohol consumption, where the reverse pattern holds. They look at imprisonment rates (higher in less equal countries), but not crime rates (just as high in more equal countries). They look at homicide, but not suicide (although here they do at least admit that suicide rates are higher in more equal countries). High teenage births are included to show that relationships in more unequal countries are often 'short-term' and 'untrustworthy', but not high divorce rates and single parenting rates, where egalitarian countries tend to perform much worse.

The measures they include are often clearly inferior to those they ignore. To measure generosity, for example, they look at government

---

6 The only rationalisation they offer, in the second edition of their book, is that they were only interested in 'problems that have social gradients', 279. I discuss this below.

spending on foreign aid, neglecting to mention that countries like the USA, UK and Australia have much higher rates of private charitable donations than more egalitarian nations. Generosity and altruism have more to do with how individuals behave than with how politicians spend taxpayers' money, so why include the donations governments make yet exclude those of individuals?

Similarly, to measure 'social capital', they use an international survey which finds that people in more equal countries are more likely to say they trust their neighbours. But there is no mention in *The Spirit Level* of data showing that people in more unequal countries are much more likely to join together with their neighbours in voluntary organisations. Again, membership of voluntary bodies is arguably a much better indicator of social cohesion than what people say in answer to a question in a survey about trust, but the latter is included while the former is overlooked. In *When Prophecy Fails*, I show it is possible to construct an index of human misery, based on indicators they neglected, which gives you exactly the opposite conclusion to the one Wilkinson and Pickett arrived at. Using this index, it is possible to show that life is much worse in more equal countries, rather than better. If you search hard enough statistics can always be found to support an argument.[7] But, as Karl Popper taught, the point of science is to try to disprove hypotheses, not prop them up.[8]

Wilkinson and Pickett have responded to this criticism by saying they only selected 'problems that have social gradients, gradients which make them more common down the social ladder.'[9]   Because rich and poor drink roughly the same amounts of alcohol, for example, alcohol consumption was not included, but drugs were included because (apparently) drug use is more common lower down the income distribution. But it is not true that they only included problems which exhibit a 'social gradient.' *The Spirit Level* happily includes indicators like government spending on foreign aid, or the number of women MPs,

---

7 As the eminent statistician, Claude S Fischer, says in his review of *The Spirit Level*: 'Anyone can easily play this game of chart-your-bad-outcomes by ransacking the websites of the UN Human Development Report, the OECD and the US Census Bureau'.   Claude S Fischer, 'Mind the Gap.' *Boston Review*, July/August 2010.
8 Karl Popper, *The Logic of Scientific Discovery*. London: Hutchinson, 1959.
9 Wilkinson and Pickett, 2010, 279.

where it makes no sense to talk of a 'social gradient', for the statistics refer to whole countries and cannot be broken down to an individual level. Nor does their response help understand why, say, imprisonment rates were included in their analysis, but not crime rates. Crime exhibits a strong 'social gradient' (both in respect of perpetrators and victims), and it is perhaps the strongest single indicator of social pathology they could have selected. So why was it left out?

Most of my 'alternative indicators' meet Wilkinson and Pickett's 'social gradient' test. Not only crime, but also suicide, divorce, single parenthood, donations to charities and membership of voluntary organisations all vary in prevalence between rich and poor.[10] It is true, of course, that they could not include everything. But why is it that every time they chose an indicator with a 'social gradient', it was one that appeared to confirm their hypothesis, rather than one that challenged it?

The use of evidence

Wilkinson and Pickett want to demonstrate the truth of their theory by taking income inequality data as their main explanatory variable. The more unequal the income distribution in a country, the worse the problems. But income distribution is a wholly inappropriate measure to test the theory they are proposing.

Their theory is about the effects of *status hierarchies*. They believe that human beings become miserable when they occupy lower positions in pecking orders, and that this is reflected in higher rates of aggression and lower levels of altruism in more hierarchical societies. To test this theory, the strength of status gradations throughout different countries needs to be compared. But Wilkinson and Pickett do not measure status gradations. They measure income differences, which are a very different thing.

This conceptual slippage between economic inequality and status differentiation becomes crucial when it is recalled that Japan plays such an important part in so many of Wilkinson and Pickett's graphs. According to their data (based on World Bank statistics), Japan has the

---

10 Fischer is particularly critical of Wilkinson and Pickett's failure to include suicide rates and single parenthood, both of which increase as we move down the social ladder.

flattest income distribution in the developed world. It also performs very well on most of their well-being and solidarity measures, so it contributes heavily to their findings suggesting that low levels of inequality produce high levels of well-being.

But Japan is far from the egalitarian culture that their analysis pretends it is. If, as their theory predicts, acute status anxiety causes human misery and social dislocation, then Japan should be scoring appallingly on all their indicators, for it is one of the most status-conscious countries in their sample. Britain's leading writer on social stratification, John Goldthorpe, has expressed exactly the same misgivings.[11] Status often stands in sharp contrast to wealth, and while some societies are stratified principally by money, others are ordered much more by status distinctions.[12] Japan is one such society, where family honour and personal shame are often far more important than how much you earn.

Wilkinson and Pickett do not appear to understand this distinction. There is only one sentence in all their rebuttals and responses that even hints that they understand this problem: 'For all its imperfections as a measure of status differentiation,' they say, 'income inequality tells us a lot about society.'[13] But the question is not whether income inequality is interesting to look at. It is whether income inequality is an appropriate measure to test the theory they are promoting. The answer, quite clearly, is that it is not.

There is, moreover, another problem with their use of evidence about Japan. Japan's income distribution may not be as compressed as Wilkinson and Pickett claim it is. They took their data on income distribution of different countries from World Bank statistics which exclude the incomes of the self-employed, farmers and single-person households – getting on for 40 percent of Japan's population.[14] The OECD includes the people that the World Bank overlooks, and it finds that far from being an economically egalitarian nation, Japan is slightly

---

11 John Goldthorpe, 'Analysing Social Inequality: A Critique of Two Recent Contributions from Economics and Epidemiology.' *European Sociological Review.* 2009, 26, 731-44.
12 Max Weber, *Economy and Society.* Volume 1, New York: Bedminster Press, 1968, 305-7.
13 Wilkinson, 277.
14 J. Bauer and A. Mason, 'The Distribution of Income and Wealth in Japan.' *Review of Income and Wealth.* 39, 1992, 403-28.

more unequal than the median (it ranks 13th on the income inequality league table of the 30 OECD nations).[15] Had Wilkinson and Pickett used these more complete OECD data, rather than the incomplete World Bank ones, Japan would have appeared around the middle of their income distribution statistics, and they would have ended up with very different graphs from those they reported.

Spurious causation

A fourth major problem with *The Spirit Level* concerns the way the authors analyse their statistical data. Throughout their book, they present their evidence in the form of simple, bivariate correlations, plotted on line graphs. Correlation and regression are common tools for analysing these kinds of statistical associations, but Wilkinson and Pickett violate many of the most basic rules and conditions of regression analysis. Because of this, many of their so-called 'findings' are invalid.

One of the major problems is that they never take account of the possible effect of third variables. Social science often finds that x and y correlate, but this may be because both are being acted upon simultaneously by a third variable. Not once do Wilkinson and Pickett test whether something other than income inequality might be producing the outcomes they plot on their graphs.

Consider, for example, their US statistics showing that the most unequal states have the highest infant mortality rates (Figure 1a). Inspecting this graph, it is immediately obvious that the most unequal states with the highest mortality rates are concentrated in the Deep South. But the southern states have higher proportions of African-Americans in their populations. There is evidence that throughout the world, women of African origin are genetically more vulnerable to early births, which are a major risk factor in infant deaths.[16] It makes sense, therefore, to check whether the high mortality rates are being produced by income inequality, or by the ethnic composition of the population.

---

15 OECD, *Growing Unequal: Income distribution and Poverty in OECD Countries*. Paris, 2008.
16 The research, reported in *The Lancet*, is discussed by Snowdon, *The Spirit Level Delusion*. Penguin, 2010, 91.

Figure 1a. Infant mortality and income inequality (US states)

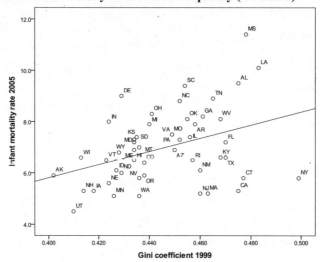

Figure 1b. Infant mortality and size of black population (US states)

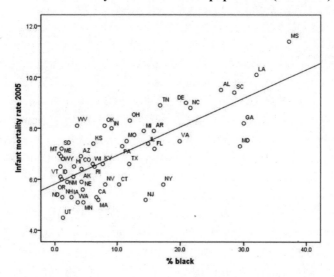

Source: Saunders, 2010, 83-6.

A simple check, Figure 1b, finds that the association between income inequality and infant mortality rates is much weaker (r=0.38) than that between ethnicity and infant mortality (r=0.74). Indeed, putting both of these hypothesised causal variables into a multiple regression equation predicting infant mortality rates shows not only that ethnicity is by far the more powerful predictor, but that income inequality fails to achieve statistical significance.

Clearly, the high infant mortality rates in the southern states reflect their ethnic composition, not their income distribution. Wilkinson and Pickett did not bother to check. They simply *assumed* that income inequality was the culprit.

To make matters worse, when I demonstrated that ethnicity is a much more powerful predictor of negative outcomes than income distribution is, they wrote an article for a UK national newspaper condemning me as a 'racist.'[17] They said it was wrong even to ask whether ethnicity might be a factor in some of the negative outcomes they had identified. In their view, it is better to publish spurious correlations than to recognise that African Americans tend to suffer higher infant mortality, homicide and teen pregnancy rates than others.

Pickett was asked why they neglected to control for third variables in a BBC Radio 4 interview in 2010. Her reply was revealing: 'You would [only] do that if you believed those variables were potential alternative explanations of the relationship you're looking at.'[18] In other words, if you do not believe ethnicity (or any other variable) might be confounding the results, then you do not have to bother checking for it. She and Wilkinson subsequently reaffirmed this extraordinary thinking in their book's second edition where they wrote: 'Including factors that are unrelated to inequality, or to any particular problem, would simply create unnecessary "noise" and be methodologically incorrect.'[19]

Their failure to check for the confounding effects of third variables was not the only serious error in their statistical analyses. They also repeatedly failed to control for the distorting effects of 'outliers.'

To demonstrate that inequality is driving the negative social outcomes they identify, Wilkinson and Pickett needed to show that these outcomes

---

17 'It is racist because it implies the problem is inherently the people themselves rather than their socioeconomic position,' they wrote. 'And that is a particularly reprehensible way to suggest inequality doesn't matter.' Wilkinson and Pickett, 'Peter Saunders's Sleight of Hand' *The Guardian Comment is Free*, July 9 2010.
18 'More or less', *BBC Radio 4*, August 27 2010, quoted by Snowdon, 167.
19 Quoted by Snowdon, 2010, 174.

are *generally* worse in more unequal countries. It is not enough to show that just one or two unequal countries score badly. To demonstrate a causal association, they need to show that most do. But in many of the graphs in *The Spirit Level*, a trend line sloping in the desired direction is achieved because it is dragged there by a unique and extreme case (often the USA for upward-sloping lines or Japan for downward ones).

The clearest example of this is their examination of international homicide rates. They report a statistically significant (p=0.025) and moderately strong (r=0.47) association between income inequality and homicides across their 23 countries. Figure 2a shows the extreme outlier in the top, right quadrant of the graph. The USA has a very high homicide rate (about 60 per 100,000), while all the other countries in their sample cluster between about 10 and 20 per 100,000. The suspicion has to be that their claim of an association between high income inequality and a high homicide rate rests entirely on this one unequal country, for it does not look like there is any such association among the other 22 countries. Without the extreme case (see Figure 2b) their apparent 'finding' collapses (r=0.03), and statistical significance disappears (p=0.159).

Figure 2a: Wilkinson and Pickett's plot of inequality against homicide rates (international)

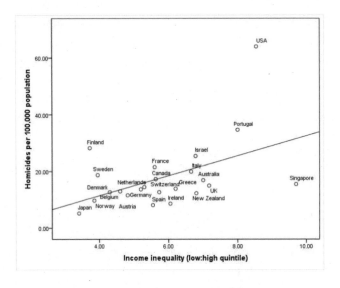

Figure 2b. Wilkinson and Pickett's plot of inequality against homicide rates, excluding the USA

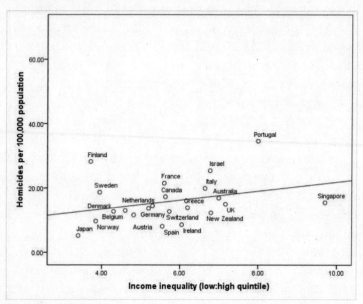

Source: Saunders, 2010, 83-6.

Nobody is denying that homicides are unusually high in the USA. The question is whether this is because of its income distribution, or because of some other distinctive factor, such as greater availability of guns. Other country data in Wilkinson and Pickett's sample suggest that income inequality cannot be the cause of the high number of murders in the USA, because all the other countries with an income distribution pattern similar to that in the USA have much lower murder rates. Wilkinson and Pickett's attribution of causation to high income inequality is spurious.

Cultural differences (an alternative explanation)

In many of Wilkinson and Pickett's graphs, the Nordic nations cluster at one end of the trend line, and the English-speaking countries cluster at the other. With four Scandinavian nations (Denmark, Norway, Sweden, Finland) and four Anglo nations (USA, UK, Australia, New

Zealand)[20] in their sample of just 23, this clustering is a major factor underpinning many of the results they report in their book.

Nobody has ever denied that the Scandinavian countries tend to perform better than the Anglo countries on the various social indicators in which Wilkinson and Pickett are interested. But the crucial question is, what is causing this divergence?

The Nordic countries have a very different history, and a very different culture, from the Anglo nations. The late industrialisation of Scandinavia (and, indeed, of Japan) means these countries still carry many of the hallmarks of a folk society. They are small, nationalistic countries where people readily identify with each other. Until very recently, they were also remarkably homogenous countries in terms of ethnicity and belief (this is also true of Japan). This homogeneity is crucial, for research indicates that popular support for state welfare spending and income redistribution weakens if people think their money is going to help people dissimilar from themselves (support for high welfare spending in Sweden, for example, has declined as large-scale immigration has increased, and the US public's antipathy to high welfare spending and income redistribution has been linked to White reluctance to support programs likely to benefit Blacks and Hispanics).[21] The homogeneity of the Scandinavian nations has thus contributed to their high level of social cohesion, and this explains their high tax and generous welfare systems.

The Anglo nations, by contrast, have a long tradition of individualism. England was a mobile, commercial country as early as the fourteenth century, when most of Europe was still stifled by a blanket of feudal ties and obligations. It then spawned the other Anglo nations – the USA, Australia, Canada, New Zealand – which, unlike Scandinavia, are all new, settler nations with young histories and remarkably diverse populations. The Anglo world has long been characterised by open borders, free trade, high rates of ethnic inter-marriage and high levels of immigration, none of which applies historically to the Nordic bloc (nor to Japan). Research demonstrates that the Anglo countries are the

---

20 Canada may be counted as a fifth, although it also has a strong French influence.
21 A. Alesina, and E. Glaeser, *Fighting Poverty in the US and Europe*. Oxford University Press, 2004.

most individualistic in the world,[22] and it is because of this that they also tend to be among the most fragmented. This in turn explains why their people tend to be distrustful of big welfare states and tax-hungry governments bent on redistributive social engineering schemes. Again, the culture explains the income distribution, not vice versa.

So is the Scandinavia-Anglo divergence which Wilkinson and Pickett pick up in so many of their graphs due to their different levels of income inequality (as Wilkinson and Pickett believe), or to the deeper, historical and cultural differences between these blocs of nations? The only way to find out is to check whether countries outside of these two blocs vary in social cohesion according to their level of income inequality. If they do, this would support Wilkinson and Pickett's claim that income distribution is, indeed, the likely cause. But if they do not, this would destroy the basic hypothesis on which *The Spirit Level* is constructed, for it would show that the book has simply picked up on the well-documented cultural differences between Scandinavia and the Anglosphere, and that income distribution is not the explanation.

In *When Prophecy Fails*, I show that, in nearly every case, when you take the Scandinavians and/or the Anglo countries out of Wilkinson and Pickett's graphs, the association between inequality and social cohesion collapses. In other words, all they have described is a cultural difference between the Scandinavians and the Anglosphere. Their hypothesis regarding the causal impact of income inequality does not stand up.

Responding to this, Wilkinson and Pickett accuse me of arbitrarily taking countries out of their analysis in order to weaken their findings. They say I 'have to remove all the Scandinavian countries' in order to destroy their finding of an association between inequality and women's status; that I 'rely on the removal' of the USA to undermine their association between inequality and obesity; that I 'have to remove both the Anglo speaking countries and the Scandinavian countries' to get rid of the association between inequality and teenage births; and so on.[23] But there is nothing arbitrary about removing the Scandinavian and Anglo countries to test whether it is their cultures or their income

---

22 Geert Hodstade, *Culture's Consequences*. Sage, 2nd edition, 2001, 215.
23 'Professors Richard Wilkinson and Kate Pickett Reply to Saunders' Pamphlet, "Beware of False Prophets", published by Policy Exchange.' *The Equality Trust* website, www. equalitytrust.org.uk (undated).

patterns that are producing the differences between them.

Wilkinson and Pickett confuse *testing for cultural distinctiveness* with the very different question of *controlling for statistical outliers*. There is a problem in some of their graphs of outliers distorting their trend lines; when this occurs, it is appropriate to remove the extreme case or cases to see whether the trend still holds. In addition, there is the separate question of whether their results are due to income distribution or cultural distinctiveness. To answer this, the cultural blocs in question – the Scandinavians and the Anglo countries – have to be removed to see if any association with income inequality remains among the other countries outside these blocs. This is done whether or not the Scandinavians or the Anglos are statistical outliers. And when it is done, Wilkinson and Pickett's results collapse like a string of dominoes.

Becoming personal

In *The Spirit Level Delusion*, Christopher Snowdon detects two principal themes in the way Wilkinson and Pickett have responded to their critics. The first is hubris: they claim their findings have been replicated so many times by reputable social scientists that they cannot possibly be wrong. They dismiss those who disagree as incompetent and ignorant. The second is wounded innocence: they claim that they are simple academics who have come under unfair attack from a well-funded right-wing conspiracy. These defences are absurd.

Snowdon has followed up their citations and finds deep disagreements between different researchers. Academics whom Wilkinson and Pickett cite as supporting them often disagree with them. Some of the most eminent researchers in the field think they are wrong. Many of these critics are on the Left, including such luminaries as John Goldthorpe, John Kay, Robert Putnam, Christopher Jencks, James Heckman and Andrew Leigh.

Wilkinson is a committed socialist. He wrote *The Spirit Level* to strengthen the traditional socialist argument for income redistribution. The question is not whether Wilkinson and Pickett, or their critics, are 'politically motivated.' The question is simply whether the empirical claims in *The Spirit Level* stand up to scrutiny.

Karl Popper should be the guide. Science, he said, involves the rigorous testing of hypotheses. It does not matter how the original conjectures arise. People become interested in topics for different reasons and might have all sorts of motives for pursuing them. Such personal details are irrelevant. All that matters is the result of the testing, for it is by testing hypotheses against empirical evidence that science gets done.

Popper went further. If conjectures are to be subjected to attempted refutations, he said, the community of scientists must be 'open.' There must be no attempt to impose a false consensus (as Wilkinson and Pickett have tried to do), and no move to exclude awkward criticisms, for it is by questioning group orthodoxies that progress in knowledge is achieved. The impetus in the scientific community must always be to try to knock down empirical claims. Those claims which survive repeated attempts at refutation are gradually accepted as probably true. Those which are refuted are thrown away.

Wilkinson and Pickett do not have much time for Popper and his method of conjecture and refutation. They want criticisms smothered. At a recent research methods seminar, Wilkinson stated: 'Scientists need a hard core to their theory that they won't allow to be refuted.'[24] Not allowing your theory to be refuted means that, if you cannot answer the critics, you have to silence them some other way. Wilkinson has sought to do this by announcing that he is unwilling to debate with me or Snowdon because our critiques were not published in peer-reviewed academic journals.[25] We apparently have no right to debate with him, for we are not 'experts' like he is: 'In other fields, people would know their thoughts were of limited value if they were not specialists: I would not dream of telling an engineer, surgeon or pilot how to do their job.' Our 'politically motivated attacks' can no longer be allowed to 'undermine science.' So Wilkinson and Pickett refuse to talk to us. And to hell with Karl Popper and the Open Society.

---

24 Quoted by Paul Jump, 'Scholars Reject Further Debate with Ideologues.' *Times Higher Education Supplement*. August 19 2010.
25 Jump, 2010.

4
When to stop government programs

Cassandra Wilkinson

Despite the fact that GDP has almost doubled in the past 20 years, we still hear our governments say that we lack the resources to invest in indigenous health, to educate our young, to care for our elderly or to protect ourselves from climate change. Tackling these problems does not require complex policy solutions; it simply requires the political will to do so.

- Richard Denniss, The Australia Institute, July 2009

Lack of accountability in grant funding entrenches disadvantage

It is often posited that the problem of disadvantage is a problem of political will by which most people really mean money. The above comment was a preamble to arguments for higher taxes to fund additional social programs. In fact, it is difficult to be sure if money is the problem because very little is known about the performance of social programs. The trend to outsourcing social work to third parties in the not-for-profit (NFP) sector has made the task of collecting evidence even more complicated.

The recent Strategic Review of Indigenous Expenditure noted: 'The strong commitments to evidence-based policy made by the Prime Minister and other Heads of Government are not matched by the quality of the evidence currently available.'[1] The report identified

---

1 Department of Finance and Deregulation, 'Strategic Review of Indigenous Expenditure.' February 2010.

many problems which are not unique to the indigenous policy sector including lack of evaluation, poor methodology and a lack of rigorous research. Without better evidence, money cannot do its job. Without better evidence all the 'political will' in the world will not make a jot of difference. Grants to the NFP sector must be reformed in a way that will improve the evidence base of public policy thereby achieving better results for the recipients of social services.

Corporatisation of welfare

The NFP sector in Australia is a significant sector of the national economy. During the 2006-07 financial year, the Commonwealth estimated the sector added $35.1 billion worth of value to the economy – about half the size of the South Australian economy and around 40 percent bigger than the Tasmanian economy.[2] The sector's growth has been driven by rising incomes, but also a trend toward transferring delivery of public social services to community organisations. Some of the transfer of responsibility has been under contract, some in the form of grants. This latter category of payments to the NFP sector is the focus of our attention. While in theory supporting non-government entities to provide services should be both cheaper and more responsive than direct public funding, many grant programs have fossilised into legacy funding streams long past their use-by date.

Government has been increasingly outsourcing program delivery to the NFP sector. While these providers arguably understand their clients' needs better than government, many programs continue to be tightly specified by the departments that issue the funding. This has led to concerns in recent years about the independence and expertise of charities being compromised by quasi-commercial relationships with governments. The effects of this have been the subject of heated discussion, largely around consequences for the independence of the sector. Critics on the political Left have been concerned about 'Silencing Dissent'.[3] Those on the political Right suggest it amounts to 'Supping

---

2 Australian Bureau of Statistics, *AUSSTATS 2008*, 2010.
3 S Maddison, R Denniss and C Hamilton, 'Silencing Dissent: Non-government Organisations and Australian Democracy.' *Discussion Paper*, Australia Institute, no. 65 June 2004.

with the Devil'.[4]

My interest is not in the strength or independence of the social sector per se but in the effects that current grant funding dynamics have had on client outcomes. Contrary to expectations, in many cases grants to NFP organisations have been neither cheaper nor more effective than public provision of services. This is not to suggest the public sector does the work better – it certainly does not. As the Finance review showed, 'Strong policy commitments and large investments of government funding have too often produced outcomes which have been disappointing at best and appalling at worst.'[5]

The difference is that grant funding involves passing the money from reasonably accountable government departments to significantly less accountable community organisations. This is not to suggest that they are generally less capable, ethical or effective – simply that the process lacks proper governance. The governance problem is compounded by the fact that charities have a superior reputation to the public and private sectors and consequently are given greater latitude in terms of demonstrated results. Roy Morgan polling on reputation for honesty and ethical behaviour finds public servants rated by respondents at 28 percent, federal MPs at 19 percent, and state MPs at 18 percent,[6] whereas *Choice* magazine has identified 'widespread support and high trust in the charitable sector' despite its survey of transparency revealing very poor levels of accountability to donors across the sector.[7]

The opaque manner in which grant programs are designed, awarded and evaluated has several problems that should be of concern to those who seek social justice:

1. The community sector remains under-funded for programs that work because it is over-funded for those that do not work

2. Clients are therefore under-serviced by programs that work and over-supplied with those that do not work, and

4 P Saunders and M Stuart Weeks, 'Supping with the Devil: Government Contracts and The Not For Profit Sector.' *Centre for Independent Studies,* 2009.
5 DFandD, 2010, 39.
6 Image of 23/29 Professions Roy Morgan Research 2009.
7 A Dooley, 'Guide to Donating To Charities: How Much of Your Donation is Gobbled Up By Fundraising Fees and Expenses?' *Choice Magazine.* April 2008.

3. Taxpayers are over-charged for programs that do not work
   and under-charged for those that do work.

While many charities are high performing, innovative and efficient, there are a large number whose funding reflects tired social theory and cosy political relationships rather than demonstrated results for the needy.

Why government increasingly uses the NFP sector to deliver services

The reasons for the growing shift in social services activities to the community sector are complex but they were largely driven by price. Government assumed that charitable donations would effectively subsidize programs and that community sector wages would remain lower than public sector wages. Outsourcing has temporarily contained growth in costs but these have come under intense pressure with the campaign to achieve parity for community sector workers. The outsourcing strategy is fast unraveling as a savings policy.[8]

There was also a sensible policy principle that tasks should be allocated to those with clear incentives to perform them well. The NFP sector is constituted, staffed and funded for social good and is, by and large, driven by the passions of dedicated volunteers and staff. Many NFPs have decades of expertise and are often closer to the grass roots of service delivery than their public service funders. Government believed it could drive its dollar further by supporting highly motivated, low cost providers to undertake important social programs.

It would have been expected, all other things being equal, that the change of service delivery would better satisfy the demand for services. However, after many years of growth in this approach, demand for human services is higher than ever. According to ACOSS,[9] there was significant growth in demand for services between 2008 and 2011. While 745 respondent organisations reported they had provided services on 6.2 million occasions in 2009-10 compared to 5.5 million instances in 2008-09, one in 20 people seeking help was turned away. This inadequacy of

---

8 ACOSS and Unions' campaign for pay parity claims 20 percent pay differential.
9 ACOSS, *Australian Community Sector Survey*. 2011.

provision is not due to a decline in grants. The Auditor-General of New South Wales estimated that, in 2006-07, state government paid $5.05 billion or 12 percent of general government expenditure as grants to external service providers. He noted this represented $750 per citizen and that grant expenditure had grown by more than 50 percent since 2000-01.

It is possible to argue, as ACOSS does, that the growth in demand reflects a need to provide more 'support for the vital sector that is left to pick up the pieces'[10] of a society experiencing increasing social dislocation due to increasing inequality. It is also possible to argue that demand is growing in spite of rising investment which suggests that NFP programs make very little difference or, at worst, are in fact contributing to, what ACOSS calls the 'growing group at the bottom'.

Unfortunately, there is little evidence to suggest any causality to prove either position. Inadequate data is collected on the results of community programs delivered with taxpayer funded grants. For all the emphasis on efficient delivery, not much is known about the effectiveness of programs and several Australian auditors-general have raised concerns about the lack of transparency that impedes assessment of the value of funded programs.

What is known about the money spent?

Auditors-general have consistently noted that governments 'cannot be sure that the grants they allocate align with their corporate objectives, and that program outcomes are achieved. This is mainly due to problems with grant selection and evaluation of results.'[11]

The Auditor-General of Tasmania examined the performance of grants to the community sector and found that advocacy rather than evidence plays the stronger role in determining who obtains grants. He further concluded that the lack of robust assessment tended to entrench established providers impeding innovation, and:

> funding to organisations has been allocated on an historical basis in both the selection of services for funding and their budgets.

---

10 ACOSS, 2011.
11 Auditor-General, *Managing Grants*. NSW Audit Office. 2002, 2.

In the past, funding was allocated on the basis of submission or lobbying and, generally, amounts provided have continued to act as a baseline.[12]

After examining 26800 grants worth \$5.2 billion, the Auditor-General of New South Wales raised a number of concerns. He concluded it was not possible to have confidence in the value of grant funded programs because the system was not well enough understood or sufficiently well managed by either those giving the money or those receiving the money.

> Only one-third of recipients said that grants are directed to areas of highest need ... In addition to this, many agencies do little to show that the public get value for money for the millions spent on grants. There are cases where grants have been given out with no follow up at all about how the grant was actually used. Clearly this is not a good way to hand out public money.[13]

He further noted that, 'while agencies publish who gets grants and how much they get, most do not publish robust evaluations that explain what grant programs have achieved and how the distribution of funds has made good use of public money.'[14]

In 2010 the Australian National Audit Office commented:

> ANAO audits of grant programs have highlighted that, in addition to promoting public confidence in the conduct of grant activities, selecting grant applications that demonstrably satisfy soundly-based selection criteria is considerably more likely to lead to a positive result in terms of achieving program objectives ... In other words, selecting the best applications promotes optimal outcomes for least administrative effort and cost.[15]

The cheapest money

The cheapest money in government ought to be that money which can be reallocated from a failing program to a successful program. Paying

---

12 Auditor-General, *Grants to the Community Sector*. Tasmanian Government Printer. 2003, 24.
13 Auditor General's Report, *Performance Audit Grants Administration 2009* accompanying press release 'Government Funds Lack Transparency', May 6 2009.
14 AG, 2009.
15 Australian National Audit Office, *Implementing Better Practice Grants Administration*. June 2010, Introduction.

for more of something that works by taking money from something that is not working ought to leave both clients and taxpayers better off.

When reviewed for value, many grants are consistently found to have failed their clients. This has not, however, prevented those same programs becoming entrenched and, over time, increasingly hard to defund. I witnessed countless examples of this dynamic in my experience both as a senior executive public servant and as a ministerial adviser.

Ministerial grants are pots of money obviously prone to discretionary allocation. They do not, however, account for the bulk of spending, most of which is undertaken on the advice of public servants who are, in their own way, as afraid of the NFP sector as the politicians. In any fight about funding government staff have insufficiently robust evidence to support their decisions and they fear that a dispute will be settled in the court of public opinion – a fight they cannot win against a charity.

While I was working for the Minister for Police the New South Wales Government hired a big four accountancy firm to review the mess of grants being allocated to a distressed inner city community. The audit found more than one hundred ongoing funding streams to NFP organisations in the area. Half of the organizations had been funded without review for so long that their original objectives were obsolete – to the point that many no longer had any clients.

Unsurprisingly the audit recommended a consolidation of funding. Unsurprisingly, the public servants recommended to the politicians that this would instigate a war on multiple fronts with the NFP organisations, each of which had an unknown number of constituents but were assumed to be reputationally superior to government and therefore likely win any ensuing media war. As a consequence, the groups retained their funding.

In NSW, funding was allocated as part of the Youth Strategy to an initiative designed to pay children in Public Housing to complete year 12. When I asked from my desk in the Premier's office for advice on how many children had taken up the grant, how many of those had in fact completed their Higher School Certificate and how many of that final group had gone on to further education or employment I was told by the Department of the Premier and Cabinet, the Office of Children and Young People, the Department of Housing and the Department of

Community Services that no such information was available. No one had established a process to monitor the grant or report on it. The lack of information did not stop them recommending that the program be extended under the next round of Youth Strategy funding.

The incoming Coalition Government in NSW has put the Better Futures program under review after years of informal advice suggested that many of its ambitions were not being met. Formal advice continued to praise the efforts of the funded groups. There is no doubt they were making efforts but results were hard to discern.

Reports like those I was seeking about the public housing students' program have been such a low priority for funders that many funded groups do not regard government review as an important responsibility. The Auditor-General of New South Wales noted:

> a significant problem across all funding programs was recipients' failure to comply with monitoring and reporting timeframes. Acquittal reports for 32% of the grants reviewed for the Ministry for the Arts and DSR were outstanding at the time of audit, being anywhere from 2 to 12 months overdue.[16]

Public and community programs fail for the same reasons – poor design, inadequate program management, limited reporting, inadequate evaluation and a lack of outcome monitoring and reporting.

The difference between this kind of failure occurring under public provision and occurring under NFP provision is that it is much harder for government to exercise authority over organisations that have greater public credibility than government itself. The more funds a NFP organisation receives, the greater the profile they can achieve. Unless they err substantially they are regarded by the media and community as a far more credible source of opinion about what is required and how to value progress than those who merely pay the bills.

The media has come to reflect the views of key elements of the sector. Many journalists treat the views of the 'underdog' charities who do not win big contracts and are regarded as not having sold out to 'corporatism' with more authority. The media also has a tendency to exacerbate the nervous instincts of politicians and public servants by

---

16 Auditor-General of NSW, *Performance Audit: Grants Administration*. 2009.

over-reacting to what are rare examples of catastrophic failure, like child deaths, and under-reacting to continuing poor performance. The former is always accompanied by calls for more money while the latter would identify key sources of those very additional funds required for the former.

Writing about the success of Job Network, Lisa Fowkes noted one of the struggles the employment service had with government was insisting on the freedom to innovate. An example was her attempt to provide job seekers with mobile phones to ensure they were informed quickly of opportunities and were easily accessible to case workers and employers. The government decided these were luxuries that should not be provided to job seekers.

A significant amount of additional prescription arose because of the government's desire to ensure that particular moral positions were reflected in the way services were delivered – either government services or positions that would withstand scrutiny by the likes of A Current Affair.[17]

While government is rarely aggressive about measuring the outcomes for program recipients, it too often interferes with the professional judgment of expert providers. A clear results-only assessment framework would have allowed Job Network to provide mobile phones providing they helped secure employment. Instead, the government interfered in process because it lacked an effective approach to outcomes.

How we might do it better

The failure of current approaches to grant funding can be attributed to a system that expects much but demands little of those who undertake social tasks on behalf of taxpayers. The Auditor-General of Tasmania advised that a better model would define measurable outputs and apply output unit costing focusing on variances in service outputs. Certainly, clearer reporting is a basic requirement of good management and accountability but I would respectfully suggest that further discussion of inputs and even outputs is not the way to resolve the problem.

An alternative is to worry less about the cost and to focus, instead,

---

17 Saunders and Weeks, 2009, 37.

on the value. A unit of care is too expensive at any price if it does not work and cheap at twice the price if it does. In the context of growing costs and opaque results, the debate about outputs and outcomes is increasingly urgent. As long as charities are paid for outputs they will focus on their own business requirements because grant acquittals will require them to have spent money as promised. As complicated as it is to transition to outcomes, it does mean that the recipient, not the provider, is the focal point for assessing value.

In an outputs world – the number of meals served, beds provided, counseling sessions delivered – the impact of the metric is ignored. Outcomes measurement requires the trickier arithmetic – days between arrests, avoided family separations, retained employment – where the impact indicates that the recipients of programs are living healthier, more engaged and socially functional lives.

With proper measurement of outcomes and robust evaluation frameworks, competing arguments about 'engineered' versus 'endemic' dependency can ascend from rough and tumble ideological street fights into informed debate. With the competing results of different programs available it is possible to see if the disadvantaged respond differently to alternative approaches of intervention and support.

The Social Impact Bond (SIB) has been developed as an instrument to put results at the centre of social contracting. Proponents hope that by doing so the pool of capital and ideas involved in social problems can be vastly increased. The SIB was an initiative of UK Prime Minister Tony Blair's Council on Social Action – a group of 'innovators from every sector' which was asked in 2007 to explore alternative models for financing social action. The NSW Government has adopted a version they are calling the Social Benefit Bond which will shortly be the subject of a pilot.

The Bond is an instrument that allows the private sector to invest in social services and to be repaid by government on the basis of demonstrated results with the financier taking the payment risk and the social provider the delivery risk. Finance for a SIB is raised on the basis that the cost of ignoring a problem is often greater than the cost of addressing it. For instance, it costs $500 per day or $182,500 per year to keep a child in prison while the social program providers attempting to stop the child going back into prison are allocated less than $5000 per year per child to keep them out.

Every admission to an emergency ward is counted by the Report on Government Services as roughly $3000. And yet programs which assist the mentally ill or homeless who make on average higher numbers of trips to hospital are often allocated less per person than the cost of a single admission. Homeless people become sick more often than those with good housing. They are also more often victims of crime. They also injure themselves more often. Ten prevented trips to hospital would more than cover the cost of roof and a bed. This is the kind of arithmetic that cannot be done without good data but it is the arithmetic that contains the solutions to many intractable social and public finance problems.

Good measurement can help move money from where it is over-invested in failed schemes to services where it is under-invested, such as keeping children out of prison. Before anyone suggests programs cannot be measured, take a look at the claims made in applications for grants. There is plenty of rich evidence cited in support of public and philanthropic funding. The task is applying that evidence to choosing sensible metrics for success.

Benefits for the sector

A contention has emerged in submissions to the Productivity Commission inquiry on Social Capital[18] that the volunteering itself rather than the good it does is an equally important point of the exercise. That is undoubtedly so in many mutual self-help organsations. For members of local civic organisations there is merit in the work even if it achieves nothing other than forming social bonds between the volunteers. For that reason I believe there should be the minimum possible administrative and regulatory burden on civil society organisations.

However, once the volunteers ask for public money rather than raising and spending their own, their efforts must be scrutinised for results. There is an opportunity cost for all public money – it could be given to someone else who will deliver the results more effectively.

---

18 Productivity Commission, *Social Capital: Reviewing the Concept and its Policy Implications*. 2003.

The grant recipient has made an implicit promise to taxpayers that they can spend those taxpayer dollars to achieve a better social result if the taxpayer had kept and spent their own money.

On May 10 2011, the Assistant Treasurer announced the establishment of the Australian Charities and Not-for-profits Commission (ACNC). While the government paper says, 'The Australian governments, the NFP sector and the public recognise that it is important the sector is well regulated so that it remains accountable to the communities it serves and that fund its diverse operations', the report is mostly concerned with 'transparency, governance and accountability.'[116] It is not concerned with results for the recipients of services. It is a producer-regulator dialogue, without the recipient (or, indeed, donor) interest being explicitly built into the evaluation design. The oft-cited concerns about the increasing burden of paperwork are true enough. As a not-for-profit director I understand the complaining. But the reality is that the accountability requirements which are onerous and largely pointless are driven by the lack of any connection to results.

If results were an explicit metric, public servants could stop harassing NFPs about how they spend their limited monies. The obsession with unit costs and acquittals is a factor the government is seeking facts rather than information because the process itself makes no sense and has no clear value. If the program were based on evidence of outcomes rather than outputs, and had clear expectations and defined goals, government could simply ask for reports on outcomes and stop tormenting the sector with paperwork about the allocated proportional rent cost of a desk in a corner and three hours a day of the manager's time to acquit the program. These things would just be the deliverer's management challenge and no business of government. Government could concern itself with the real questions: 'what would work for your clients?'; 'were original assumptions changed to make the program work?'; 'what lessons have been learned and how is new knowledge applied to get a better result?'

The Productivity Commission proposals to improve regulation are concerned with regulating process and have little likelihood of

---

19 Department of Finance and Deregulation, *Establishing a Regulator for the Not-for-Profit Sector.* 2011, 10.

influencing outcomes. They certainly will not support innovation or provide impetus to build on each organisation's core mission. Writers on both the Right and Left have worried that coporatisation of the NFP sector risks undermining the unique mission and purpose of charities leading to a range of problems including mission drift, disconnection with members and a loss of social capital.[20] This sort of analysis often misses the point in that it is not for the sake of government that service providers must improve their performance but rather for the sake of clients.

The transition of NFP organisations into government sub-contractors, however, does raise serious problems. NFPs can less effectively challenge the wisdom of government approaches to social problems. This impedes innovation, debate and improvement. I have worked with NFP organisations whose evaluated programs suggest their internally designed, philanthropically funded projects have clearer benefits than their government designed publicly funded programs. If this is the case more broadly than I have observed, important lessons for program design and delivery are missing. Peter Shergold made the observation that:

> The prime advantage of contracting non-profit organisations to deliver government services should be the opportunity to stimulate social innovation. It's not just that community based organsiations can produce outcomes more effectively than public service agencies but that collectively they can trial new, more service oriented methods of delivery.[21]

Another serious concern about the use of NFP organisations as sub-contractors to government is the erosion of product differentiation between the charities. A clear mission and unique perspective informs each group's approach and is an invaluable recruiting tool for volunteers. If volunteers, funders and supporters of charities begin to believe they are just arms of the government, this is likely to have detrimental effects on the health of the sector and on civil society more broadly.

---

20 H Irvine, K Lazarevski, and S Dolnicar, 'Strings Attached: New Public Management, Competitive Grant Funding and Social Capital.' *Faculty of Commerce – Papers.* University of Wollongong, 2009.
21 Saunders and Weeks, 2009, 63.

The reason many charities exist and draw support is that they bring their unique moral, social and professional perspective to the task of making the world a better place. Donors or volunteers seek to propagate their values and align to organisations whose theory of the challenge is compelling and whose expertise and perspective appears to be well-placed to implement change. For instance, to ease hunger a donor may choose between a fair trade based charity, or a religious based charity, or a medically skilled charity. Over time it should be possible to compare the efforts of these different approaches to see whether hunger was most successfully ameliorated by medical, economic or pastoral methods.

There is so much to gain from allowing competing approaches to flourish. A rich marketplace for services for the needy based on competing efforts to deliver measurable results would be a radical change, one that just may work where traditional approaches continue to fail.

5
Closing the Aboriginal gap is not socially just

Wesley Aird

... the strongest foundation for achieving greater access to social justice for Aboriginal and Torres Strait Islander peoples is to ensure that all policies, programs and legislation are underpinned by:

- *Our right to participate in decision-making that affects our lives*
- *Our right to the principle of free, prior and informed consent, and*
- *Your duty to consult and negotiate with us in this process.[1]*

    - Mick Gooda, Aboriginal and Torres Strait Islander Social

    Justice Commissioner, 2010

In contemporary Australia there is frequent discussion about human rights. When a discussion of human rights involves Indigenous Australians, it is common to invoke the notion of 'social justice'. An early explanation was provided by Mick Dodson, when he was the first Social Justice Commissioner:

> ... social justice is about getting up in the morning. It is also about the opportunities you have during the day and the way you feel when you put your kids to bed at night. It is as basic as the routine or struggle of day-to-day existence. Every person has reasonable

---

1 Mick Gooda, Aboriginal and Torres Strait Islander Social Justice Commissioner, speech entitled 'Social Justice and Aboriginal and Torres Strait Islander Peoples Access to Services.' *QCOSS Regional Conference.* August 12 2010.

expectations of basic standards of living.[2]

Somehow, as Mick Gooda attempts to declare in the opening quote above, Indigenous people now invoke the notion of 'social justice' as some sort of veto over delivery of government services. The new usage of the term 'social justice' is very loud on rights but silent on responsibilities. 'Social justice' has been turned into a transaction that is all about money.

For more than a decade the notion of 'social justice' has enjoyed immense popular support through the reconciliation movement and, more recently, an enormous array of social campaigns such as the Getup! Close the Gap[3] campaign and the campaigns of Oxfam Australia[4] and Amnesty International.[5] This ideology has been well and truly embodied by the Rudd and Gillard governments, packaged as the Closing the Gap Initiative at which they have thrown billions of dollars. No matter how big the budget, government cannot overcome someone else's disadvantage, nor can a community do it – it is always up to the individual.

What in the common prescription does not work to solve indigenous disadvantage?

Of the estimated 517,000 Indigenous Australians in 2006, some 75 percent lived in major cities or regional areas.[6] Entirely consistent with Pareto's Principle (also known as the 80-20 rule whereby roughly 80 percent of the effects come from 20 percent of the causes[7]) and, for reasons I cannot fathom, the overwhelming focus of Indigenous

---

2 Mick Dodson, 'Land Rights and Social Justice.' In Galarrwuy Yunupingu (editor) *Our Land is Our Life*. University of Queensland Press, 1997, 39.
3 The Close the Gap campaign supported achieving Indigenous health equality within a generation.
4 Oxfam is 'committed to the ability of Aboriginal and Torres Strait Islander peoples to freely determine their own political, economic, social and cultural development is fundamental to realising their rights.' And also to, 'helping Indigenous Australians realise their right to self-determination.' http://www.oxfam.org.au/explore/indigenous-australia/our-aboriginal-and-torres-strait-islander-peoples-program/self-determination-program
5 See http://www.amnesty.org.au/indigenous-rights/?
6 Productivity Commission, *Overcoming Indigenous Disadvantage 2011*. 2011, 2.
7 Based on the observations of Italian economist Vilfredo Pareto, who observed in 1906 that 80 percent of the land in Italy was owned by 20 percent of the population.

programs is aimed at the minority living in remote and very remote centres.

Instead of making difficult choices (for instance, to cease supporting particular services in a particular locality), governments endlessly tie up communities in rhetoric and consultation. For example, '[s]ome 25 percent of Indigenous Australians live in locations classified as 'remote' or 'very remote', in many of which the multiple dimensions of Indigenous disadvantage are starkly evident. While the need for policy intervention in these communities is clear and compelling, a key consideration is the long-term economic viability and sustainability of a community.'[8]   As a result of the inability to place choices on the policy agenda, no decisions are made that would resolve the future of remote communities, and all Indigenous Australians suffer from ill-conceived policy regardless of whether they live in the outback or an inner city.

The causes and prescription for disadvantage share strong similarities among racial or cultural groups all over Australia. In 2006 just over 98 percent of the Australian population lived in major cities, inner regional and outer regional areas;[9]   higher standards of service can be achieved in the provision of mainstream services. The majority of Indigenous people live within the major cities and towns. Disadvantaged Indigenous people are, however, discouraged from seeking assistance from mainstream service providers. They are instead directed to Indigenous-specific services which may well be niche but they cannot match the standards of the mainstream providers.

For decades successive governments of the Commonwealth, states and territories have provided many billions of dollars towards Indigenous-specific programs. For whatever reason, possibly for fear of a social backlash, programs have not been designed to achieve value for money. As popular as this ideology may be, it has failed to overcome Indigenous disadvantage. In 2010 the Department of Finance formed the view that, '[p]ast approaches to remedying Indigenous disadvantage have clearly failed, and new approaches are needed for the future.'[10]   And also that,

---

8 See Department of Finance, *Strategic Review of Indigenous Expenditure*, February 2010, 15.
9 Productivity Commission, 2011, 2.
10 Department of Finance, 2010, 11.

The Commonwealth's total expenditure on its Indigenous specific programs amounts to some $3.5 billion annually. This major investment, maintained over many years, has yielded dismally poor returns to date.[11]

In 2011 the Productivity Commission stated:

[i]n a few areas, the gaps are narrowing. However, many indicators show that outcomes are not improving, or are even deteriorating.[12]

These statements reveal very plainly that the Closing the Gap ideology is not the solution that is going to deliver improvements in the lives of Indigenous Australians. The Closing the Gap campaign may have the numbers on its side (whether that be people, dollars, or both), but it is doomed by weak ideology and no accountability.

Why does it not work?

The Closing the Gap ideology does not work because it does not focus on the disadvantage of an individual or the services available to that individual. Instead, it creates a false division along racial lines and expects Indigenous people in need to attend their local Indigenous-specific organisation to engage in the theatre of consultation and to receive so-called 'culturally appropriate' services. For many years Indigenous affairs at the federal level has been centred on a particular department, more recently with the Department of Families, Housing, Community Services and Indigenous Affairs (FaHCSIA). Complementary Indigenous-specific services are provided by other departments, for example, the Department of Education, Employment and Workplace Relations or the Department of Health and Aging. In the current machinery of government, FaHCSIA's responsibility for Indigenous matters aligns with the current political ideology. Even though the politics and the Department are aligned, this is the wrong response to the problem. It serves instead to perpetuate disadvantage rather than to overcome it.

The political ideology is founded on the appearance of achieving

---

11 Department of Finance, 2010, 11.
12 Productivity Commission, 2011, 3.

engagement as if, on its own, engagement is necessary and sufficient to overcome disadvantage; this contributes to the failure. The importance of engagement is demonstrated in the National Indigenous Reform Agreement (NIRA), agreed by COAG in November 2008, which sets out the *Service Delivery Principles for Programs and Services for Indigenous Australians.*[13]

The second of the six principles is the 'Indigenous engagement principle'. It states that, 'Engagement with Indigenous men, women and children and communities should be central to the design and delivery of programs and services'. In other words, engagement appears to be the end goal rather than just a tool to be used along the way. Sadly, this is the epitome of the 'social justice' message, particularly in the Closing the Gap era.

As an example of the rhetoric, the media release by the Indigenous Affairs Minister, Jenny Macklin, in response to the *Overcoming Indigenous Disadvantage Key Indicators 2011* stated, '… Government cannot close the gap alone. Closing the Gap requires a genuine partnership with Indigenous Australians at all levels and the Government is committed to a relationship based on trust and mutual respect.[14]

The Minister's media release is very much 'on-message', that engagement is the critical factor in overcoming disadvantage. For some reason this only applies to Indigenous Australians. One can only imagine how unpopular a minister would be if, for instance, Centrelink or services for the homeless were overhauled entirely on the advice of their customers. Such an approach would be patently unacceptable for mainstream Australians, yet there seems to be a very real policy perspective that Indigenous disadvantage is somehow different to any other sort of disadvantage.

Apart from the usual business of consultation, there are many indicators of valuing engagement over actual achievement – the apology to the stolen generations; endorsement by the Rudd Government of the United Nations Declaration on the Rights of Indigenous

---

13 Council of Australian Governments, *National Indigenous Reform Agreement.* 2008.
14 The Hon Jenny Macklin, Media Release, August 25 2011.

Peoples;[15] establishment of the National Congress of Australia's First Peoples;[16] or commitment to constitutional recognition. Given the plight of Indigenous Australians, these symbolic gestures should not be allowed to distract the government from the difficult task at hand. There is no evidence that these gestures assist to close the gap. The sustained focus on symbolism creates an unreasonable sense of entitlement thereby driving up demand for Indigenous-specific services which do not deliver positive outcomes.[17] However, to overcome disadvantage Indigenous people must access the best possible services available to them; in most cases these will be mainstream rather than Indigenous-branded.

The failure to harness mainstream services in a coordinated manner has significantly contributed to the failure of the Closing the Gap ideology. There is an apparent lack of willingness and rigour in application of funds in a coordinated manner throughout all levels of government. Instead, Indigenous-specific funds are allocated without meaningful regional needs analysis or meaningful regard to other assistance schemes (mainstream or otherwise) operating in the vicinity. Making the most of mainstream services is a particularly wicked dilemma for the Commonwealth given the very substantial portion of services delivered at the local level by State or territory agencies. This point is not lost on the Department of Finance:

> A major role for the Commonwealth under the new COAG framework should be to hold States and Territories to account for their delivery of those mainstream services for which they are responsible (especially in critical areas such schooling, health, housing, community services and related infrastructure). Where mainstream programs and services fail to deliver their intended results the appropriate policy response should be to reform those mainstream services rather than to create a new array of ad hoc

---

15 For reasons against endorsement of the Declaration refer to Senate Hansard No. 10 2007, September 10 2007, 53 and in particular the speech by Senator Marise Payne.

16 For examples of its reception refer to Noel Pearson quoted in D Jopson, 'New Indigenous "Company" Structured to Keep Politicians at Arm's Length.' *The Age*. May 3 2010 and also Warren Mundine quoted in P Karevelas, 'Congress is a Waste of Money, says Warren Mundine.' *The Australian*. April 27 2011. Congress has also been described as no more than a "club" by Marcia Langton, quoted by Karevelas, 2011.

17 Refer to Department of Finance, 2010 and Productivity Commission, 2011.

funding programs.[18]

Rather than focus on services and outcomes, the Commonwealth's Closing the Gap Initiative has resulted in a bewilderingly complex 'strategic framework' including three inter-connected priority outcomes, six national Closing the Gap targets with twelve headline indicators and the seven strategic areas for action and the accompanying strategic change indicators.[19] It is its own bureaucracy within the bureaucracy. To make matters worse, the convoluted Initiative ties up funding and service delivery at all levels of government and out into de facto service providers such as Indigenous corporations. The National Indigenous Reform Agreement was agreed by COAG in November 2008. It commits all jurisdictions to achieving the Closing the Gap targets.[20] The Department of Finance, however, concluded in 2010 that 'there are real risks that the States and Territories will not deliver on key aspects of the agreed COAG agenda.'[21]

One of the more egregious outcomes of the Closing the Gap campaign and, indeed, the transactional nature of self-determination, is that Indigenous people in well-funded Indigenous organisations have been allowed to wield great power over other Indigenous people through application of taxpayer funds without accountability. This is entirely consistent with the international experience of oppressed group behaviour as described by Paolo Freire in 1970: 'It is a rare peasant who, once "promoted" to overseer, does not become more of a tyrant towards his former comrades than the owner himself'.[22]

What alternative may work better?

For non-Indigenous Australians involved in the fight to overcome disadvantage there exist highly complex mechanisms to analyse in great detail the social and economic influences and then to develop equally detailed service responses. It is about time Indigenous Australians had access to the same level of sophistication instead of being relegated

18 Department of Finance, 2010, 28.
19 For a detailed explanation see Productivity Commission, 2011, 2.2.
20 http://www.fahcsia.gov.au/sa/indigenous/progserv/ctg/Pages/NIRA.aspx#a_1
21 Department of Finance, 2010, 14.
22 P Freire, *Pedagogy of the Oppressed*. Penguin Books, revised edition 1996, 28.

to 'culturally-appropriate service' which is usually a euphemism for 'service of a lesser standard'. The following sections contain my proposed alternatives for overcoming Indigenous disadvantage, set out in three main categories; national, urban and remote.

National

Nationally, Indigenous people need, and are entitled to, the option to choose the best possible service available. Services should be local and should not be segregated by race.

Mindful that generalisations do not make for effective service delivery, Tony Vinson[23] has demonstrated that disadvantage can be mapped to provide 'statistically reliable and consistent information about every population centre.'[24] The broad categories used by Vinson were: social distress; health; community safety; economic; education. Each category had within it four to eight indicators. In Vinson's assessments the number of indicators employed varied between 20 and 25 depending on the circumstances of each locality.[25] The results of this or any similarly robust exercise could assist support agencies to deliver services in an integrated manner to people in need. The importance of understanding the distribution of disadvantage is an enormously powerful tool in the fight to overcome it and the information is available for service responses to be based on the local circumstances and the local opportunities. No Indigenous funding should be supplied where high quality services are accessible by another provider.

It is time to remove Indigenous institutions that do not deliver services at the same standard as their mainstream counterparts. To be clear, I recommend abolition of separate Aboriginal and Torres Strait Islander corporations where these entities do not have the same compliance expectations as an entity established under mainstream corporations law.[26] With a history of poor regulation, it is not surprising governance issues and complaints of poor behaviour and cronyism

---

23 T Vinson, *Dropping off the Edge*. Jesuit Social Services and Catholic Social Services Australia, 2007.
24 Vinson, 2007, vii.
25 Vinson, 2007, 6, table 2-1 breaks the indicators into 6 main groups.
26 Refer to Office of the Register of Indigenous Corporations, *Comparative Table of Commonwealth, State and Territory Incorporation Legislation*. March 2008.

plague these corporations. The sheer quantum of money poured into Indigenous corporations through various grants programs risks the organisations (or, more pointedly, the humans running them with little if any accountability) to perpetrate oppressed group behaviour on the very people they are funded to help.

The abolition of these entities should deliver two critical benefits. Firstly, the government will not have a 'false crutch' to use Indigenous organisations as de facto service providers – a role for which they are sadly ill-prepared. Secondly, individuals that are Indigenous but not members of an Indigenous entity will no longer be 'invisible' to the bureaucracy. Where consultation is legitimately required on a particular service issue it should reach all individuals, not only the stakeholders in the 'Indigenous Industry'.

It is time to pull the plug on the Closing the Gap campaign. It has had the effect of promoting Indigenous exceptionalism. Each and every Australian, irrespective of race or culture, should participate in our society on the same social contract. In broad terms, Australia is a country in which its citizens enjoy a high standard of life and, by extrapolation, a high standard of enjoyment of human rights. Indigenous rights do not confer a power of veto over the mechanisms of good governance. The pendulum needs to swing back somewhat to a point where there are both rights and responsibilities.

Urban

For urban Indigenous Australians my proposal is to put an end to the debilitating policy consequences of the Pareto Principle. There should be an end to government administration developed for the minority of people in remote communities that ends up being applied across the board to the cities and towns where it simply does not work. Urban Indigenous Australians should be encouraged to see that true 'social justice' is achieved when we stop being a passenger and start being a participant. To translate this into action, there must be an end to the 'Indigenous Industry' in which Australian society has accepted a lesser contribution from Indigenous people and this has resulted in Indigenous people being maintained at the bottom of the socio-economic ladder.

Sadly, being a passenger is promoted by the notion that 'social justice' is somehow reliant on Indigenous people having separate representation; the Aboriginal and Torres Strait Islander Commission (1990-2005); and, since 2010, the National Congress of Australia's First Peoples. In his report on the consultation which lead to incorporation of the National Congress, Tom Calma stated: 'The discussion about a new National Representative Body is about our place at the table in making the decisions that impact on our communities, on our men, our women and our children.'[27] This is a pernicious form of cargo cult that encourages individuals to shun personal responsibility, always thinking that someone else will solve their problems.

Being a participant in society is about taking responsibility for our own lives, one household at a time. The way it should happen is the parents go to work (to the extent of their capability) and the children go to school – the same social contract as the rest of Australia. Counter-intuitively, this model respects culture and cultural affiliation because with education and employment comes choices such as the choice of association. When you are down and out, you do not have choice.

In any community where there is a strong desire to work collaboratively, Indigenous people should be assisted to develop social ventures[28] and social entrepreneurs.[29] In every instance there should be encouragement for positive change that supports culture and business.

Remote

In 2006, more than 80,000 people lived in the 1,112 discrete Aboriginal and Torres Strait Islander communities in remote areas of Australia.[30] It is inconceivable that each and every one of these communities is sustainable because no amount of taxpayer money can sustain passive, socialist communities. For those communities that have the potential to be sustainable, initiatives should build the capacity of individuals whilst also breaking away from the socialist mindset.

27 T Calma, in the *Report of the Steering Committee for the Creation of a New National Representative Body*. Human Rights and Equal Opportunity Commission, 2009, iii.
28 See for instance *Social Ventures Australia*.
29 For instance as described by Andrew Mawson in *The Social Entrepreneur*. London: Atlantic Books, 2008.
30 Australian Bureau of Statistics, *Australian Social Trends*, 2008.

Government cannot decide which communities are sustainable. Government must respect the vital role to be played by community members planning their own future. The role of government is to make an informed investment decision and to cease the practices of the past that have ended up in dysfunction and waste. In many communities the most valuable contribution the government can make will be to do less. Communities that end up being sustainable will be those where a group of individuals, supported by (but not run by) government, have both the will and the capacity to succeed. Conversely, where a community cannot guarantee proper standards of living, the government has an ethical responsibility to withdraw support.

Critical to the sustainability of communities is a process of creative analysis by which a group of community champions makes it their objective to make the community sustainable. Rigour in this process can be achieved by using a modified form of the Logical Framework Approach or a similar analytical aide. It is an analytical process, but it need not be onerous; for instance, a community plan could be developed in a matter of days with help from a technical facilitator.[31]

A process such as the one that follows is critical for all communities. If a community has the benefit of, for example, a viable service industry or a native title benefits package, then a community plan is critical in setting out how the community can derive maximum benefit lest the money will be squandered. Where a community does not have an economic base, an objective plan is essential to help the residents plan for relocation to a place or places where there are jobs, education, services and utilities. The major steps are set out below.

To make a start, it takes a small group of community champions to define broadly their idea of the beneficiaries of their efforts and also to set out any assumptions upon which they are relying. At this early stage it is most important to identify the community's needs, the problems (both apparent and core) as well as the cause and effect relationships. As Chester Porter has written, 'The whole point is that the solution of a problem is usually not hard; it is the defining of the problem that is

---

31 See for instance, AusAID, *AusGUIDElines*. 2003; J Hampshire, *The Logical Framework Approach – Guidelines.* February 1999; C Saldana and J Whittle, *Using the Logical Framework for Sector analysis and Project Design.* Asian Development Bank, 1998.

more difficult.'[32]

The next critical step is to decide the objectives of a community plan. This is where the community makes a concrete statement about the standards of living they want for themselves. Having set the standards, it will become apparent where, and how much, the community needs help.

It is then relatively simple to list the stakeholders and also their potential working relationships. A simple analysis of each stakeholder will also provide valuable clues as to how each stakeholder can contribute to overcoming the problem. Some stakeholders will be asked to contribute, whereas others will be asked to stay away. The next step is to list and prioritise the activities to be done by each stakeholder and also how these will be monitored.

With the activities incorporated in an implementation plan it will be necessary to identify any threats, whether these are organisational, philosophical, bureaucratic or personal, and so on. Each threat should be assessed for its probability and effect. The other key parts of the plan will be how to revise the plan or activities during implementation and also how the plan is communicated within the team and to the stakeholders.

Only at this point is the government able to make an informed decision as to whether or not the community has the will and the capacity to deliver a proper standard of living for its members, and only at this point should the government make a decision whether or not to invest in the community. From here the principles of good governance and service delivery swing into action. For most, this process will not be easy, but it will deliver a better standard of living.

The process in the preceding paragraphs is novel to Australia. It is, however, based on practices that have been in use for decades by most of the world's international development agencies. Whilst the process provides objectivity it cannot guarantee the sustainability of a community where, for instance, there is neither an economy nor genuine community participation. In the absence of these, a community is unlikely to be able to guarantee an appropriate standard of living for its residents and, as stated earlier, the government has an ethical

---

32 C Porter, *The Gentle Art of Persuasion*. Random House Australia, 2005, 74.

responsibility to withdraw support.

Conclusion

For the last four decades Indigenous affairs has seen the rise of 'social justice' ideology alongside constant increases in funding without accountability. But the three very significant government reports released in 2011 have made plain that the old ideology simply has not worked. It is time to realise that if the gap cannot be closed with $3.5 billion per annum, then it cannot be closed with the Closing the Gap ideology. It is time for all Australians to live on the same social contract. We can overcome Indigenous disadvantage and we can do it one household at a time.

6
Dysfunctional parents damage their children

Jeremy Sammut[1]

The current emphasis in policy and practice is to keep children with their families wherever possible. Where children, for various reasons, need to be placed in out-of-home care, the practice is to attempt to reunite children with their families.[2]

'Removing a child is a last resort,' a caseworker says. 'Quite often we try not to remove the child.' Another call comes in and this one is even more disturbing. A four-month-old baby's head has been slammed into a concrete pylon because the parents are intoxicated and unable to walk properly. The parents are already known to welfare workers and three of the baby's siblings are in foster care.[3]

For those on the Right of the political spectrum, child protection is a difficult issue because the Right places a premium on limited state intrusion into the lives of individuals. The Right also defends the sanctity of the private world of the family and is wary of the potential violation of this realm and abuse of power by capricious state authorities.

Despite these reservations, child protection reform that upholds the

---

1 This chapter is based on Jeremy Sammut, 'The Power and the Responsibility: Child Protection in the Post-Welfare State Era.' *CIS Occasional Paper 117*, Sydney: The Centre for Independent Studies, 2010a.
2 Australian Institute of Health and Welfare, *Child Protection Australia 2008-09*. 2010, 36.
3 'On the Road with DoCS Crisis Response Team', *The Daily Telegraph*. June 10 2011.

independent rights of children needs to be on our agenda because we live in a world the Right did not make. The Right did not champion the 'right' to unconditional welfare, which has arguably entrenched poverty in disadvantaged communities. Nor did it press to extend the role of the state into more and more aspects of civic life arguably at the expense of voluntary effort and civil society. However, all taxpayers have to live with and pay for the destructive personal, social and political consequences of the rise of the welfare state, which includes the terrible impact on the lives of increasing numbers of children.

Child protection policy and practice failures deny vulnerable children the emotional security, the educational opportunities, and the proper parenting all children need. These failures create the next generation of abusive and neglectful parents. For those concerned about the size of the welfare state and maximising the freedom of all citizens, breaking the intergenerational cycle of neglect and abuse is essential to contain the growth of the state and extra-state entities that 'bottom feed' on the misery and waste of potential caused by child abuse and neglect. The paradox is that greater intervention is needed in the lives of dependent members of the community to save future generations from lifelong dependence. The broader cultural issue is whether the Right has the will to defend core community standards, or whether the morally and ideologically questionable perspectives of the Left will continue to dictate social values in so important an area as child protection.

The system

The clientele of child protection services predominantly consists of members of the underclass. The underclass is that proportion of the non-Indigenous and Indigenous population who are long-term welfare dependent, and have a range of welfare-dependence induced and exacerbated behavioural issues, such as domestic violence and substance abuse, which are very hard to resolve. The complex and often intractable problems these families experience include the inability to parent children adequately and serious concerns for child well-being.

The social services catering for underclass families are mainly provided by social workers and other counsellors employed in or funded by government social service departments. These departments are plagued by the waste and other problems typically found in heavily-unionised, politically-cosseted bureaucracies. Child welfare laws grant these departments the statutory authority to remove vulnerable children in danger of abuse and neglect from the custody of their dysfunctional parents. But they are failing to fulfil their statutory responsibilities because, in too many child safety cases, the presumed right of dysfunctional parents to keep possession of children is elevated above the rights and best interests of children.[4]

Traditional child protection work – the statutory investigation of child welfare reports by caseworkers trained to assess whether a child is in need of court-approved removal from the family home and alternative care arrangements – has been marginalised owing to the culture of non-intervention in family situations. While encouraging parents to change their behaviour and meet children's needs has always been a part of modern child protection, the pendulum has swung too far in recent decades towards trying to fix broken families and giving parents almost 'limitless opportunities' to change.[5] Social service bureaucracies provide family-centred, rather than child-centred services, to allow biological parents to retain custody of children, even where children are identified as being in imminent danger of harm. Children are only removed from parents as a last and reluctant resort.[6]

The Left and parental 'rights'

The preoccupation with preserving parental custody is typical of woolly-minded thinking about rights typically found on the contemporary Left. The idea that welfare-dependent heroin addicts have a 'right' to keep their children in housing commission squalor reveals a particular kind of ideological confusion.[7]

---

4 Jeremy Sammut, 'Fatally Flawed: The Child Protection Crisis in Australia.' *CIS Policy Monograph No. 97* Sydney: The Centre for Independent Studies, 2009a.

5 Chris Goddard and Joe Tucci, Responding to child abuse and neglect in Australia. A join submission to the Australian government responding to Australia's children: Safe and well – a national framework for protecting Australia's children (Melbourne: Child Abuse Prevention Research Australia, Monash University, 2008, 8.

6 Australian Institute of Health and Welfare, *Child Protection Australia 2008–09.* 'Chapter 5: Intensive Family Support Services.' *Child Welfare Series No. 47,* 2009.

7 See, for instance, Human Services Community Services, *Working with Parental Substance Misuse, Research to Practice Note.* Sydney: NSW Government, February 2010.

The moral judgments that sound child protection depends on are beyond the comprehension of all who accept the kind of Leftist cultural politics promoted in some sections of academia. In 2009, Kate Murphy, Marian Quartly, and Denise Cuthbert accused those who frown on drug-addled parenting of supporting the 'conservative family policy of the Howard era.'[8] This form of minimisation of a serious social problem would be bad enough if it only reflected the dated ideology pervasive in child protection, which is that removing children punishes poor parents who are helpless victims of structural socio-economic injustice.[9] This sentiment lies behind the commitment to family preservation at almost all costs which dominates thinking and practice in the child and family welfare sector. A misplaced egalitarianism prevails. The belief that parental capacity has been unfairly distributed across socio-economic groups explains the desire to 'redistribute' parental capacity via government-funded support programs.

Worse than this unrealistic faith in the ability of social service interventions to rehabilitate highly dysfunctional parents, however, are the post-modern values that have seeped into mainstream thinking in the field. They cast child protection as a moral panic deployed to authorise the social surveillance and cultural oppression of the powerless and excluded.[10] The far-fetched notion given credence by Murphy, Quartly and Cuthbert is that child welfare laws hold parents to 'socially constructed' behavioural standards to buttress the hegemony of traditional 'bourgeois' family values. Treating parental intravenous drug use in a relativist manner, as if drug-addled parenting is somehow a legitimate, alternative lifestyle choice, is wrong and dangerous; it denies the reality of child abuse and neglect.

---

8 Kate Murphy, Marian Quartly, and Denise Cuthbert, "'In the Best Interests of the Child": Mapping the (re) Emergence of Pro-Adoption Politics in Contemporary Australia.' *Australian Journal of Politics and History*. 44(2), 2009, 201–218.

9 For the 'welfare paradigm' and critique, see John Frederick and Chris Goddard, 'Exploring the Relationship Between Poverty, Childhood Adversity and Child Abuse From the Perspective of Adulthood.' *Child Abuse Review*. 16(5), 2007, 323–341.

10 Jacques Donzelot, *The Policing of Families*. New York: Pantheon, 1979.

The Right and children's rights

Those on the Right need not hesitate out of misplaced doctrinal concerns to make judgments about the rights of parents as against the rights of children. When the welfare of children is at stake, it is not 'too harsh' or illiberal to hold parents accountable for bad behaviour in circumstances that obviously contravene John Stuart Mill's famous principle that liberty should only be interfered with to 'prevent harm to others.' Mill himself argued that it was in the case of children 'that misapplied notions of liberty are a real obstacle to the fulfilment by the State of its duties.'[11]

Mill was one of the nineteenth century progenitors of the progressive idea that a child had the right to enjoy his or her full liberties and opportunities as a future citizen. In *On Liberty*, he argued that parents who failed to fulfil their 'sacred duties' towards their children were guilty of 'a moral crime both against the unfortunate offspring and against society ... if the parent does not fulfil this obligation, the State ought to see it fulfilled.'[12]

Because the Left dominates so many areas of contemporary social policy, the Right's long, if interrupted, history of enlightened social activism on behalf of vulnerable members of the community is often overlooked. The international child protection movement, which developed in Britain and spread to the United States and Australia in the late nineteenth century, was – like the movement to emancipate women – a project inspired by the enlightened ideas found in the writings of Mill.[13] Active citizens joined together to form philanthropic societies devoted to advancing the care and protection of children from bad and inadequate parents.[14]

The state empowered these voluntary associations of citizens by setting out the legal framework for their activities – the original child welfare laws – which permitted child protection societies actively to

11 John Stuart Mill, *On Liberty*. Cambridge: Cambridge University Press, 1989, 105.
12 Mill, 1989, 105.
13 George Behlmer, *Child Abuse and Moral Reform in England, 1870-1908*. Palo Alto: Stanford University Press, 1982.
14 Cliff Picton and Peter Boss, *Child Welfare in Australia: An Introduction*. Sydney: Harcourt Brace Jovanovich, 1981, 21.

seek out and rescue children from unsafe homes. But the state did not crowd out voluntary effort to protect children.[15]

Since the 1970s, however, the near-to-total governmentalisation of social services in Australia has crowded out this tradition. Too much has been left to be done, badly and at great cost to children and society, by the state and its agents. The 'new class' of bureaucrats and Left-leaning social workers and other professionals employed in government departments have won the war to exclude ordinary citizens from involvement in child welfare and have retained, by and large, the exclusive right to identify and treat abused and neglected children in their preferred family-centred fashion. The bureaucrats, together with assorted academics, 'helping' professions, and 'charitable' organisations, continue to shape the system to suit their own interests, rather than to meet the needs of the most vulnerable children in the community.

Contested causes

Amid all the scandals that have engulfed child protection systems in virtually all Australian jurisdictions during the last 20 years, the irony is that their one undoubted strength – the mandatory reporting of child abuse and neglect – is singled out as the greatest weakness.[16]

Police, education and health professionals in all states and territories are legally obliged to report their concerns when they suspect children are at risk of harm. Leading academic commentators argue that mandatory reporting has failed to protect children better because, instead of promptly identifying the most serious cases of abuse and neglect, as was intended, it has led to the enormous growth in the number of reports due to 'over reporting' of 'less serious' cases. Swamped child protection services, critics say, are unable to respond to the most serious reports of child maltreatment because they are distracted by the administrative task of sifting reports. To reduce the burden and deal with less urgent cases, 'stakeholders' urge governments to make additional funding

---

15 For this history, see Dorothy Scott and Shurlee Swain, *Confronting Cruelty: Historical Perspectives on Child Protection in Australia*. Melbourne: Melbourne University Press, 2002.
16 Adele Horin, 'Time to Have the Little Children Suffer no More.' *Sydney Morning Herald*. March 7 2009; Caroline Overington, 'Foster Care in Response to Child Abuse Harmful.' *The Australian*. November 17 2008.

available to provide more family support services.[17]

The Cashmore submission[18] is a very influential account of the causes of the child protection crisis but is not supported by evidence; instead, it is based on myths that serve the agendas of key interest groups in the child protection policy debate.[19]

Far from the failure it is made out to be, mandatory reporting has worked very well.[20] The expanding underclass has been mass-screened; the heightened surveillance of dysfunctional families has driven the growth in the number of reports; and the children most at risk have been identified and re-identified, mostly by mandatory reporters.[21]

The real problem is the quantity and quality of basic child protection work. There is a vicious cycle of under-responding to reports concerning 'known' children; this creates high levels of unmet need. A hard core of frequently re-reported vulnerable children and dysfunctional families account for large proportions of the child protection reports. But despite report after report of serious concerns for child wellbeing, many of these children are not even 'seen' by a caseworker.[22] Even when investigations occur, and even in cases where abuse and neglect are proven, the action taken (if any) is often inadequate, and too many children are left in dangerous situations.[23]

Academic-activists, with past practices and controversies in mind, argue that the yawning gaps in the system are small mercies because keeping dysfunctional families united is better than separating children

---

17 Judy Cashmore, Dorothy Scott, and Gillian Calvert, 'Submission to the Special Commission of Inquiry into Child Protection Services in NSW.' also titled 'Think Child, Think Family, Think Community: From a Child Protection System to a System for Protecting Children.' NSW Commission for Children and Young People. March 2008.
18 Cashmore, Scott and Calvert, 2008.
19 Andrew McCallum, 'Child Protection and Wood: Will we Rise to the Challenge?' *Developing Practice*. 23 Autumn/Winter 2009, 4–6.
20 Ben Matthews and Donald C. Boss, 'Mandated Reporting is Still Policy with Reason: Empirical Evidence and Philosophical Grounds.' *Child Abuse and Neglect*. 32, 2008, 511-516.
21 Sammut, 2009a, 13-14.
22 The Hon. James Wood, AO, QC, 'Report of the Special Commission of Inquiry into Child Protection Services in NSW.' Sydney: Government of NSW, 2008, ii-iii; Ombudsman Victoria, *Own Motion Investigation into the Department of Human Services Child Protection Program*. Melbourne: Ombudsman Victoria, 2009.
23 Northern Territory Government, *Growing them Strong, Together: Promoting the Safety and Wellbeing of the Northern Territory's Children, Report of the Board of Inquiry into the Child Protection System in the Northern Territory*. Darwin: Northern Territory Government, 2010, 257.

from their biological parents.[24] No one is denying the pain that separation from birth parents can cause even if parents are incapable of meeting their children's basic needs. But what is worse is children being abused, neglected and killed while the massed ranks of the welfare state hesitate at the front door of the family home.[25]

This is no exaggeration. Professor Chris Goddard, Director of Child Abuse Prevention Research Australia, and Joe Tucci, Chief Executive of the Australian Childhood Foundation, have pointed out that in the contemporary welfare state, dysfunctional parents 'can have drug and alcohol workers, domestic violence workers, mental health workers, homelessness workers, family support workers' – every conceivable service and a long history of involvement with many government departments, except a skilled child protection worker to monitor the family situation in the best interests of children.[26]

The result is high numbers of repeat notifications concerning vulnerable children with well-founded and continuing safety concerns. In 2008-09, 60 percent of the risk of harm reports the NSW Department of Community Services received were re-reports, an average of 1600 re-reports each week.[27] Despite a $750 million 'reform' program implemented in January 2010 designed to strengthen the focus on family support and relieve the pressure on the statutory system, only a small proportion of reports in NSW – around three percent according a leaked internal report – are receiving a response that includes a face-to-face home visit by a child protection caseworker.[28]

The problem is not confined to NSW. A report prepared by the Victorian Ombudsman in November 2009 found that more than 2,000 children, or almost one quarter of all reported children, had no allocated Department of Human Services caseworker.[29] The response by the department – whose total budget rose by 163 percent between 1999 and

---

24 Kate Gaffney, 'Apology to Wards of the State Reflects our Collective Regret.' *The Age.* October 29 2009.

25 NSW Ombudsman, 'The Death of Ebony: The Need for an Effective Interagency Response to Children At-Risk.' Sydney: NSW Ombudsman, 2009, 51.

26 Chris Goddard and Joe Tucci, 'Sins of Omission.' *The Australian.* July 15 2008.

27 Albert Zhou, *Estimate of NSW Children Involved in the Child Welfare System.* Department of Community Services. 2010, 2-3.

28 Jane Hansen, 'Report Exposes DoCS Failure.' *Sunday Telegraph.* January 9 2011.

29 Ombudsman Victoria, 2009.

2009[30] – has been to close cases without investigation to appear to meet (on paper) 'allocation' targets; this has led to the same children being re-reported 'months later with much worse instances of abuse.'[31] The proportion of reported children the subject of a substantiated finding of abuse or neglect and subject to a re-substantiation within 12 months ranges from 10 percent and 14 percent in Western Australia and Victoria respectively, approximately a quarter in Queensland and the Northern Territory, one-third in NSW, South Australia, and Tasmania, and more than half in the ACT. The rate of re-substantiation has either increased or held steady in most states and territories in the last decade.[32]

From statutory to support services

The explanation for this parlous state of affairs is systemic. Institutional and ideological changes during the last 40 years have led to major shifts in policy.

By the 1980s, child protection in all Australian states was carried out by university-trained professionals employed in centralised state government agencies set up to receive and respond to reports.[33] These agencies were, and remain, sub-departments of complex 'community services' departments in all states and territories. The orthodox theory and practice in these bureaucracies is that the best way to keep vulnerable children safe is to construct a vast social service system to assist dysfunctional parents keep and regain custody of children. The social workers, psychologists and drug counsellors who deliver these services, whether they work for the government or for charitable organisations, have little interest in traditional child protection work but have a vested interest in keeping children with their parents to justify the provision of taxpayer-funded support services. Importantly, an Allen Consulting Group report published in 2009 found that charitable non-government organisations (NGOs) were 'wholly supportive' of plans to continue to shrink the role of the statutory child protection services and wholly in

---

30 Milanda Rout, 'Kids in Crisis Slip Through Cracks.' *The Australian*. October 20 2010.
31 Milanda Rout, 'Pressure to Close Child Abuse Cases.' *The Australian*. October 19 2010.
32 Productivity Commission, 'Report on Government Services 2011.' Canberra: Productivity Commission, 2011, Table 15A.10.
33 See Leah Bromfield and Prue Holzer, *A National Approach for Child Protection: Project Report, National Child Protection Clearinghouse.* Australian Institute of Family Studies, 2008, 12–14.

favour of expanding the role of out-sourced family support services.[34]

The non-interventionist and virulent anti-adoption thinking that holds sway is not evidence-based. It has failed to reduce abuse and demand for statutory protection.[35] The studies that show this approach is misconceived also reflect a terrible truth: dysfunctional people stay damaged ... and damage their children. But the prevailing ideology rules out the logical path to a better future for these children despite the role that family preservation plays in facilitating child harm.[36]

As the 2005 House of Representatives inquiry into adoption in Australia concluded, the evidence showed that at-risk children who are removed early, speedily and permanently have better outcomes compared to children who are 'temporarily' removed and cycled through multiple foster placements and failed family reunions, as currently occurs in thousands of cases.[37] The detrimental impact of episodic foster care is cited as further proof that family preservation is preferable.[38] This is a false reading of the situation. It is not surprising that children become disturbed when shuffled in and out of family and foster homes, and are denied the stability and attachment every child needs to thrive. In fact, good quality foster care, involving a permanent placement, and a one-on-one relationship with trusted carers – all help to repair disturbed children.[39]

Yet the debate about child protection policy mainly occurs on another plane removed from the realities on the ground and the unsatisfactory outcomes for children. The debate about the Stolen Generations, and whether Australian governments removed thousands of Indigenous children for racist reasons or safety concerns, is among the most heated

---

34 Allen Consulting Group and Australian Research Alliance for Children and Youth, 'Inverting the Pyramid: Enhancing Systems for Protecting Children.' Melbourne: Allen Consulting Group, 2009, 48.

35 Sammut, 2009a, 16.

36 Chris Goddard and Joe Tucci, 'Secretive System Doesn't Bear Scrutiny.' *The Australian.* November 18 2008.

37 House of Representatives Standing Committee on Human and Family Services, *Overseas Adoption in Australia: Report of the Inquiry into Adoption of Children from Overseas.* November 2005, ix, 126.

38 Karen Healey, 'Critical Questions about the Quest for Clarity in Child Protection Regimes.' *Communities, Children and Families Australia.* 4(1), 2009, 52–58.

39 Successworks, 'Evaluation of the TRACK Program.' Victoria: Department of Human Services, 2005.

public controversies in Australia.[40] Many personal and family tragedies resulted from removal of Indigenous children. We should never forget or repeat the trauma experienced by the members of Stolen and the Forgotten generations who were mentally, physically and emotionally damaged by institutionalisation and for which the nation is truly sorry.[41] Well-meaning governments therefore prefer temporary removal to permanent removal for fear of standing accused of stealing and forgetting another generation. Yet the contemporary practice is damaging an increasing number of children and has prompted the suggestion that future Australian governments may have to apologise all over again, this time for failing to remove at-risk children.[42]

Notwithstanding the focus on preventing removals, rising numbers of Indigenous and non-Indigenous children are in out-of-home care (OOHC) for welfare reasons.[43] Increasing numbers of these children have serious psychological and behavioural problems caused by abuse and neglect experienced prior to their eventual removal as a last resort. These problems are exacerbated by the instability subsequently experienced in care due to foster placements breakdowns caused by children's 'high and complex needs'.[44] Many have been in care for years and could have and should have been adopted years earlier.[45] Yet there are pitifully few 'local adoptions' in Australia each year.[46]

Out-of-home care is the most expensive part of the child protection system and accounts for two-thirds of total national spending on child and family welfare.[47] The escalating cost creates a financial disincentive

---

40 Keith Windschuttle, 'The Fabrication of Aboriginal History.' Volume Three, *The Stolen Generations*. Sydney: Macleay Press, 2009; Robert Manne, 'Aboriginal Child Removal and the Question of Genocide' in A. Dirk Moses (editor), *Genocide and Settler Society: Frontier Violence and Stolen Indigenous Children in Australian History*. New York: Berghahn Books, 2004.

41 Australian Senate, *Forgotten Australians: A Report on Australians who Experienced Institutional or Out-of-Home Care as Children*. Canberra: Government of Australia, 2004.

42 Jeremy Sammut, 'Some Kids Really Need to be Rescued.' *The Australian*. November 18 2009b; Chris Goddard and Joe Tucci, 'In Victoria, Another Forgotten Generation in the Making.' *The Australian*. December 7 2009.

43 Productivity Commission, *Report on Government Services 2011*. 2011, Table 15A.16.

44 See Jeremy Sammut, 'Do Not Damage and Disturb: On Child Protection Failures and the Pressure on out of Home Care in Australia.' *CIS Policy Monograph No. 122*. Sydney: The Centre for Independent Studies, 2011.

45 AIHW, *Child Protection Australia 2009-10*. 2010, Table 4.6.

46 AIHW, *Adoptions Australia 2008-09*. Child Welfare Series No. 48. 2010, 25.

47 Productivity Commission, 2011, Table 15A.1.

for governments to refocus on traditional child protection work for fear of placing even more children into the stressed OOHC system (there is also a national shortage of volunteer foster carers).[48] The only affordable and sustainable way to provide safe and stable homes for all the children in Australia who need permanent protection is by removing the official taboo placed on adoption by family preservation-focused child welfare agencies. Enabling suitable families to adopt from out of care those children who have little prospect of safely returning home would alleviate the pressure OOHC expenditure is putting on government budgets and be a major step toward addressing the systemic problems that impede effective child protection.

The fog of politics

The huge gaps in core statutory child protection practices have been identified in independent reports compiled by the Ombudsmens' offices in both NSW[49] and Victoria.[50] But rational analysis has not led to rational policy solutions – more and better investigation of reports and more permanent removals in the best interests of children. Traditional child protection work remains marginalised because policy outcomes are subverted by the appalling interest group-driven politics in the sector.[51]

The politics of child protection proves the old saying that yesterday's solution is tomorrow's problem. Since the mid-1980s, the recommended policy response to government social service failures has been to outsource delivery of these services to NGOs. The theory was that outsourcing would infuse taxpayer-funded programs with the volunteer ethic of the charitable sector.[52] In practice, according to the free-market economist Henry Ergas, the attempt to revitalise civil society has empowered 'self-appointed, but taxpayer-funded, guardians of the public interest, whose only difference from other rentiers is that they are

---

48 Pia Akerman, 'An Infant Dead, a System at Fault.' *The Australian*. April 19 2008.
49 See, for example, NSW Ombudsman, *Report of Reviewable Deaths in 2006 Volume 2: Child Deaths*. Sydney: NSW Ombudsman, 2007, iv–v.
50 Ombudsman Victoria, 2009.
51 Jeremy Sammut, 'The fog of child protection politics.' *CIS Policy*. 26(2), 2010b, 41.
52 Peter Saunders and Martin Stewart-Weeks (editors), 'Supping with the Devil.' *CIS Policy Forum No. 16*, Sydney: The Centre for Independent Studies, 2009.

more vocal and intransigent.'[53] This is especially true regarding child protection. The experiment with outsourcing has created new political complications that frustrate sound reforms, work against balanced provision of social services, and distort policy and funding priorities.

Policy-makers are intensively lobbied about child protection policy by peak organisations representing the charitable sector, principally concerning the distribution of public funding as opposed to how best to meet the needs of children. To achieve leverage over policy-making, lobbyists conduct media campaigns which repeat many untruths about the problems in the system, and make many promises about the benefits of a family support-oriented system, that fly in the face of the evidence. Governments and Oppositions are urged to support the family preservation approach on the condition that the delivery of support services is outsourced. State governments pursue this path and fund the charitable sector at the expense of re-focusing the system on delivering responsive, traditional child protection services.[54]

Post-welfare state solution

The 'fog' created by the politics does not, however, obscure what really needs to be done to improve the situation for neglected and abused children. We need stand-alone child protection agencies that are:

- Staffed and led by child protection specialists
- Rigorously assess and forensically investigate 'risk of harm' notifications to assess whether statutory action to remove children is required
- Operated as the lead agency in coordinating, supervising and monitoring the response to child protection matters by developing child-focused service plans
- Able to 'buy in' targeted support services, if appropriate, to give parents a 'first and last chance' to clean up their act, based on best practice decisions concerning the family situation and the needs of children, and
- Are held accountable by independent statutory officers and by public reporting of transparent data.

---

53 Henry Ergas, 'Maggie Showed Keating the Way.' *The Australian*. January 12 2010.
54 Sammut, 2010a.

Politicians mandating a new policy direction in children's best interests could achieve meaningful child protection reform. Sustained political leadership would see politicians say publicly and unequivocally that the effort made to preserve and support dysfunctional families is doing more harm than good. Responsible ministers would drive cultural change in child welfare agencies and ensure the fervent belief in the superiority of the family preservation approach is superseded by the principle of early removal and adoption. Politicians would have to act untrue to type, to an extent, and would have to respect the evidence, stare down the ideologues and lobbyists, and not be content any longer to preside over a continuing disaster and spin their way out of periodic crises.

There are, hence, many reasons to believe that politicians are likely to take the line of least resistance and to be pessimistic about governments implementing the change that is required. This is especially so considering how resistant social service bureaucracies are to change, and given the extent to which policy formation is driven by noisy interest groups, influence-peddlers, and rent-seekers throughout all parts of government. Many ministers and shadow ministers confuse 'inclusive' policy-making with thinking it is their job to satisfy the vested interests in their portfolio. They are prone to defer to the NGOs and recycle uncritically what they are told about the need for more government funding for family support, which keeps happy the loudest and best organised voices in the debate and minimises negative media coverage.

The solution is to circumvent the politics. Citizens dissatisfied with the status quo should demand the right to reclaim the system from the politicians and bureaucrats unwilling or incapable of ensuring that child protection is done properly. Child protection failures should be dealt with as extreme cases of failed bureaucratic service provision and the 'capture' of public policy by vested interests. Child protection needs a radical reorganisation based on classical principles of citizenship and civil society to allow those on the Right to have a direct say in the proper governance of the system.

The bureaucracies should be closed down as the failed institutions they are. Their statutory responsibilities should be assumed by reconstituted child protection societies. Each society would be established by statute, be membership-based, and have its own elected, independent board. The board would hire the management team and frontline caseworkers. The budget of each society should be determined by Parliament and be supplemented by subscriptions and other fundraising activity. The board would have full financial and operational control over the budget subject to standard corporate probity requirements. The society's statutory charter would be to fulfil the key roles of a stand-alone child protection agency outlined earlier State governments would regulate through a state-wide inspectorate agency – but not run the societies.

A most important advantage of a de-bureaucratised, citizen-controlled system would be that the political dynamics would be revolutionised. At the moment, few individuals or groups are actively engaged in lobbying government in the best interests of the children in greatest need. Child protection societies would permanently unite public-spirited citizens willing and able to advocate on their behalf. They would also fill one of the biggest gaps in the current system – the knowledge gap. Public interest in child protection is only occasionally sparked when another disaster or damning report hits the headlines. Governments respond to community outrage with the standard spin about doing more to support families. Then it is back to business as usual.

This is the pattern because the outrage is as ignorant as it is impotent for want of practical experience. The governmentalisation of child protection has not only centralised power over the system but also centralised control of knowledge. Ordinary citizens unfamiliar with the system find it difficult to challenge what they are told about how it should and should not be run. A dearth of informed debate is the result. Myths such as over-reporting and the need for more family services fill the vacuum. This would change if disinterested and well-versed citizens armed with valuable and ever-increasing corporate knowledge were intimately involved in the running of child protection societies.

Conclusion

A defeatist objection readily comes to mind. Even if responsibility for child protection is devolved to civil society, will not the membership and boards of child protection societies be dominated (eventually if not immediately) by the same ideologues, lobbyists and their fellow travellers who will decide that too much family preservation is never enough? This is a genuine but unavoidable risk that those interested in reclaiming child protection from the Left have to take. The point of devolving responsibility for child protection to ordinary citizens is to give those on the Right the chance to recover their heritage of enlightened social activism in keeping with Mill's idea of the rights of the children, conscious of all the challenges and frustrations this will involve in a plural society.

Restoring the role of the Right in child protection may not therefore be an appealing prospect, based on practical rather than philosophical considerations. This most probably amounts to asking people to spend time in meetings arguing with Leftists who think the drug-addled have a right to raise children 'with appropriately funded support services.' But reluctance to get involved, while understandable, is not an option because there are worse things. What is worse for the welfare of children is letting those on the Left escape unquestioned, unchallenged and unaccountable, in defiance of the evidence that reveals how badly children are being failed by current policy and practice. Hence those on the Right must join the fight on children's behalf. And we should do this in civil forums where right thinking about children and their needs can prevail.

7
Churches, charities and community development

Ruth Limkin

Cindy visited our charity's offices recently. As a single mother with a two year old daughter, finances were tight, and she needed some assistance from our Fresh Start Food program. Cindy's first food parcel was brought out to her. While clearly grateful, she also appeared uneasy as she looked through the goods. The reason for her discomfort soon became apparent when she picked up the rolled oats, and quietly asked if the instructions to make porridge came with pictures. Cindy could not read or write and she had never been shown how to cook porridge. It was a stark reminder that Cindy's physical poverty was the outworking of a greater social poverty which included relational isolation and educational disadvantage. Sadly, it was poverty also likely to make its effects felt far into the future.

Someone should do something

Common to an Australian understanding of community is the desire to help our neighbour. Good people wrestle with how best to address poverty and disadvantage, and to help people such as Cindy and her daughter practically. Decision-makers have long seen the provision of cash benefits, through the social security system, as an effective solution to poverty and disadvantage. Since the Second World War, there has been a considerable increase in the types of welfare payments available to Australians. These are now virtually embedded within our economic landscape.

In addition, government social workers are often tasked with playing a preventative or direct intervention role in families experiencing deterioration or dysfunction. This is particularly the case where children are in disadvantaged families. Interventions are designed to ensure at-risk children have the educational, nutritional and health outcomes commensurate with families experiencing comparative advantage or in a higher socio-economic area. Noble as those intentions are, however, even a short survey of the state of current Australian society leaves us sobered by the seeming lack of constructive difference that such responses have made.

The Young Australians and Social Inclusion study was released in 2011 by the Australian National University. It outlined the disadvantages experienced by young people who were raised in households which were heavily dependent on welfare for more than six years. The disadvantages included poor education, difficulty finding employment, poor relationships with parents or no relationship with their father, and social exclusion. Quite simply, the receipt of welfare alone has failed to alleviate poverty and disadvantage, particularly for children of welfare-dependent households.

Commenting on the study, Commonwealth Families Minister, Jenny Macklin, explained that the government wanted to 'support these parents to finish school, get new skills and find employment, so that they can build a strong future for themselves and their children.'[1]

Education and employment are important to reduce disadvantage. In order to build a strong future for children, however, attention must also be paid to the family structure, and the prevention of its deterioration or dysfunction. The recent release of the National Survey of Family Growth highlighted the benefit of resilient, intact families for children's health and development. The project, by The Centre for Disease Control, cited studies which asserted that 'children in cohabiting families tend to perform worse in school and be less psychologically healthy than those whose parents are married.'[2] It also quoted a 2010 report by the US Department of Health and Human Services which found that 'children

---

1 Renee Viellaris, 'Welfare-Dependent Parents Set Their Children Up For Failure.' *The Sunday Mail.* August 21 2011.
2 Sabrina Tavernise, 'More Unwed Parents Live Together, Report Finds.' *The New York Times.* August 16 2011.

living with two married biological parents had the lowest rates of harm – 6.8 per 1000 children – while children living with one parent who had an unmarried partner in the house had the highest incidence, at 57.2 per 1000 children.'[3]

W. Bradford Wilcox, associate professor of sociology at the University of Virginia, and director of the National Marriage Project, said of the survey: 'There's a two-family model emerging in American life. The educated and affluent enjoy relatively strong, stable families. Everyone else is more likely to be consigned to unstable, unworkable ones.'[4] Strengthening family units makes social sense. With individuals and the broader community bearing the long-term emotional, mental, physical and economic costs of family deterioration and dysfunction, preventative programs become an imperative response, albeit an expensive one. The cost of preventative family interventions is considerably difficult to measure, although estimates using the limited data available calculate the cost in Australia in 2007-08 at approximately $1.16 billion.[5]

Research continues to show that strengthening marriages and reducing parental conflict is in society's long-term public health interest. In September 2011, the Australian Christian Lobby released a report by Professor Patrick Parkinson, of the University of Sydney. The report, *For Kid's Sake: Repairing the Social Environment for Australian Children and Young People*, quoted Professor Paul Amato, who said:

> Research clearly demonstrates that children growing up with two continuously married parents are less likely than other children to experience a wide range of cognitive, emotional, and social problems, not only during childhood, but also in adulthood. Although it is not possible to demonstrate that family structure is the cause of these differences, studies that have used a variety of sophisticated statistical methods, including controls for genetic factors, suggest that this is the case.[6]

3 US Department of Health and Human Services, 'National Incidence Study of Child Abuse and Neglect', cited in Tavernise, 2011.
4 Tavernise, 2011.
5 P Taylor, P Moore, L Pezzullo, J Tucci, C Goddard, and De Bortoli L, *The Cost of Child Abuse in Australia*. Melbourne: Australian Childhood Foundation and Child Abuse Prevention Research Australia, 2008.
6 P Amato, 'The Impact of Family Formation Change on the Cognitive, Social, and Emotional Well-Being of the Next Generation.' *The Future of Children*. 15(2), 2005, 75-96.

In addition to the cost of preventative measures, governments carry considerable expense incurred from their direct interventions in family dysfunction. Since 2004-05, the amount spent on intensive family support services has increased, on average, more than 37 percent per year. The Productivity Commission's 2010 Report on Government Services states that $2.2 billion was spent nationally on child protection and out-of-home care in 2008-09.[7] Quite simply, with such substantial increases in costs, there is a sobering economic reality facing those who design and implement policies to strengthen families. With Australian governments facing very real limitations on personnel and finances, it is possible that, without changes, the costs of government intervention and prevention measures may prove unsustainable.

We the people

Who will care for and strengthen the nation's families? Are there ways in which communities can assist individuals and strengthen families, and do so in a more integrated, less bureaucratic manner than at present?

> When government accepts responsibility for people, then people no longer take responsibility for themselves.[8]
>
> - George Pataki, former Governor of New York, 1995-2006

Something remarkable happened in Brisbane in the summer of 2011. People remembered what it meant to live as a part of community. As floodwaters rose, inundating more than 20,000 premises, so rose community spirit. When the waters receded, tens of thousands of volunteers descended upon affected suburbs to clean, organise and remind victims that they were not alone. Councils mobilised quickly yet lacked the resources to assist every individual property comprehensively. In the end, it was the kindness of strangers that helped to clean a city.

As repair and restoration of individual properties lay far outside the scope of government responsibility, the council call centre became a conduit rather than a destination, connecting those in need with volunteers ready to help. This may have simply been a hastily cobbled

---

7 L. Bromfield, P. Holzer and A. Lamont, 'The Economic Costs of Child Abuse.' Australian Institute of Family Studies, *Fact Sheet*. April 2011.
8 http://c250.columbia.edu/c250_celebrates/remarkable_columbians/george_pataki.html

together arrangement, necessitated by the sheer scale of the event and the response it required. It may also have been a glimpse, however, of an effective model for future community development, through the mode of community engagement.

During the post-flood recovery phase, while governments were criticised for the way red tape was delaying assistance to flood-affected families, local churches and charities were praised for their rapid grassroots response. One reporter described them as 'sophisticated local networks'.[9] It is not just in natural disasters that community and faith voluntary organisations are known to be successful. They are also generally regarded as being highly effective in development and delivery of services, by reason of being more connected to the communities they serve when compared to those from the government sector.[10]

Additionally and interestingly, there is a particular benefit of faith organisations in mobilising community response – whether in disasters, community issues or long-term development. This is due to the fact that they have an existing membership that is already engaged, and a leadership and communication structure that enhances the capacity to respond effectively.[11] It is little wonder that even dedicated governments compare poorly with these 'sophisticated local networks' in enhancement of community development and provision of service delivery. In a research project which looked at the role of the community sector in welfare responses, a policy level stakeholder from a local government area said:

> [I don't think the answer is] government programs or so called engagement structures like forums ... I'm not saying there isn't a role for the state obviously, both the local and central government is a vital role ... But it seems to me that if you're talking about creating more positive communities and empowering communities to address their problems, that's more likely to come from their organisations that they've created, that are embedded in the

---

9 Michael Madigan, 'Charities and Churches More Effective at Disaster Relief than Queensland Government.' *The Courier-Mail.* June 21 2011.
10 UK Department for Communities and Local Government, *What Works in Community Cohesion.* June 2007.
11 DCLG, 2007, 50.

community, than from some top down structure.[12]

Further, as community organisations are most likely to be intimately acquainted with the nuances and needs of the community in which they live, they are 'best placed to understand how to tackle problems, more likely to be trusted, and better able to engage with key sections of the community.'[13]

Positive communities require a high level of community cohesion, or 'interdependence and solidarity between members of a society', which relates to the 'connections and relationships between individuals, groups and organisations within a community.'[14] According to the Affordable Housing National Research Consortium, the absence of community cohesion means 'segments of the community will experience social exclusion; in effect they will be prevented from full participation in the life of the community.'[15]

In *Fighting Chance: Tackling Britain's Gang Culture*, Patrick Regan, youth worker and founder of British youth charity XLP, addressed the importance of grassroots community engagement and mentoring to build community cohesion and reduce social exclusion. After the London riots in August 2011, Regan spoke about some systemic, underlying issues in the community which contributed to the angst and social fracture evidenced in the widespread rioting and destruction. Regan said:

> There's a real issue of role models here. We did a scheme a couple of years ago where we took 20 kids, all on the verge of exclusion. We recruited 20 volunteers in the local community and said, 'Give them two hours a week, life coaching, support them, text them, get to know their family, help them create life goals. After a year, 18 out of those 20 kids are still in education. One went back to Africa and one truly dropped out. Ninety percent of them had refrained from anti-social behavior. So it shows that change is possible, but you do need to invest in the right places and take a long-term view of it.[16]

---

12 DCLG, 2007, 49.
13 DCLG, 2007, 49-51.
14 L. Holdsworth and Y. A. Hartman, 'Indicators of Community Cohesion in an Australian Country Town.' *Commonwealth Journal of Local Governance*, volume 2, 2009, 76-97.
15 Holdsworth, 2009, 76-97.
16 Deutsche Welle News Service, (undated).

Mentoring is long-term, intensive work which requires considerable investments of time, so rigorous assessment of such a model is important from a pragmatic perspective. One Australian model of comprehensive, long-term family support is COACH. This program, the acronym of which stands for creating opportunities and casting hope, relies on individual mentoring for families rather than forensic intervention by government employees. In this long-term mentoring program, which takes a community development approach to alleviating poverty, trained volunteer coaches are paired with families who have at least one child in primary school and who identify as needing assistance.

The twelve month program provides opportunities for coaches and clients to meet regularly, often weekly, for one to three hours. Through structured intake interviews, and evaluation requirements, the coach-client pairing works through areas of life that the family would like to see improvement in, and can involve parenting skills, nutrition, finding employment, budgeting or other areas of concern.

Monash University, in its initial evaluation of the COACH program, found that the patterns of 'working side by side' with clients helped to 'encourage the development of their clients' social independence'.[17] The evaluation continued: 'This kind of help, working alongside is quite different from a welfare mentality that expects coaches to solve clients' problems for them. Instead: they [coaches] are giving them [clients] responsibility for their actions.'

Evaluation from 2010 indicates significant benefit to those involved. The Victorian program site, which was assessed, provided support to 37 families with 76 children. The families evaluated their mentoring experience, and reported the following ways in which the mentor or program assisted or encouraged them:

- 89 percent received general emotional support, practical support or education to manage stress, anxiety or anger
- 70 percent were better able to manage their housing, including locating housing, rental or mortgage arrears advocacy, developing maintenance or cleaning routines, or

17 T. Gale, E. Peeler and B. Jane, *COACH Community Mentoring Evaluation*. Faculty of Education, Monash University, April 2006, 34.

generating income for payment of rent

- 73 percent had improved family cohesion, through better communication and problem solving, education and accessing family therapy or counseling
- 59 percent had stabilised their mental health through maintaining links with services and encouragement to adhere to medical advice
- 38 percent had improved community support links by accessing community managed social groups and recreational activities, and
- 76 percent had new insight or a greater ability to manage their finances.

In terms of family support, a community engagement model such as this is a cost-effective way to see positive change. One worker can support approximately five or six client-coach relationships per day of weekly employment, which means a full-time worker will facilitate a total of 60-90 contact hours each week.

Engaging volunteers effectively, within the delivery of a strategic program, enhances community welfare in a variety of ways. The worth of volunteers goes beyond simply building social capital or community cohesion, particularly when they are trained to engage in strategic program delivery. In fact, volunteers contribute significantly to the nation, with their value to Australian charities being estimated at $14.6 billion annually.[18] Those who receive the services provided by trained volunteers benefit greatly, and the volunteers themselves also receive benefits.

A recent article on volunteering cited a number of studies that showed the benefits of volunteering to participants.[19] These included improved mental health, with 61 percent of people who volunteered at least five times a year reporting that these activities assisted them in feeling less stressed. Other studies showed that volunteering reduced depression for those over 65. Interestingly, the article states that for the elderly, 'volunteering on religious grounds is more beneficial than

---

18 Commonwealth of Australia, Office for the Not-for-Profit Sector.
19 Sara Fernandez and Ray James, 'Volunteering for Happiness and Health.' *Australian Health Promotion Association.* (undated).

volunteering for secular reasons.'

When a community cares for itself, it also nourishes itself. When we accept responsibility for ourselves, and our neighbour, we begin to build a cohesive and constructive approach to eliminating disadvantage, exclusion and poverty. We may well be the answer to someone else's prayer, and in the very act of helping, also answer our own.

The politics of partnership

I count it a privilege to assist those in our community who are experiencing disadvantage. The few staff and many volunteers who administer our programs are commendable, yet everything they do occurs within a framework established by those who partner with us.

When Cindy and her daughter came to collect the food parcel, we could help her only because of the nexus between government, business and our not-for-profit organisation. Without these relationships, the service would be either entirely limited, or non-existent.

For example, while we have given out crisis food parcels for many years, we have recently redesigned them and redeveloped the program. It is now a medium term support program which includes a number of initiatives that provide people with the information and education they need to improve their nutritional intake and eating habits.

The parcels themselves are now nutritionally balanced, and contain ingredients for a week's worth of healthy meals. Our community nutritionist, has formulated a weekly meal plan based on the core components of the food parcel, recipes are included with the parcel each month. Cooking classes will assist those who have not yet learned how to prepare a meal from scratch, as well as providing important opportunities to reduce social isolation and encourage community interaction.

A significant hurdle faced in redesign and implementation of this program was how to ensure that clients had access to fresh fruit and vegetables. With limited budget capacity, purchasing fresh produce was beyond us, particularly considering its variable price and shelf life. When talking to a local business with a significant chain of stores, however, we discovered that they were eager to donate excess fresh stock to us. In a serendipitous moment, just as we approached them, a recent change in legislation had reduced their risk in donating excess food for charitable activities. Not only were we able to increase the quality and quantity of the food parcels for our clients significantly, but we were also able to link them to another charity that had a similar need.

When Cindy received her food parcel, it was the happy result of a cooperative partnership between government, business and the not-for-profit sector. I suspect such partnerships are the key to long-term, effective community transformation.

Community organisations can develop tailored solutions and mobilise volunteers, the corporate sector can assist with provision of goods and services, and the government can create a legislative environment which promotes, enables and rewards such partnership.

As XLP founder, Patrick Regan, said:

> We live in the communities ... so we must have an incredible knowledge of the issues... We have tailor-made solutions, but we can't do it on our own. I said to the deputy prime minister yesterday: 'You need to help us. You need to help some of the good practice, things that are going on the ground that are changing peoples' lives. You need to help us be able to scale up.[20]

The idea of governments helping the community sector to 'scale up' or build capacity has gained traction during the past decade. In 2006, the Community Business Partnership, set up by the then Prime Minister of Australia, John Howard, commissioned research to follow up from a study in 2000 regarding trends in corporate community investment.

The resulting report stated that:

> in relation to corporate community investment, Australian governments have been active in endorsing, facilitating and partnering ... Indeed, there is a very strong trend in government itself, endorsed by public policy theorists and leading practice, to engage business and communities more deeply in the core business of government ... This trend is characterised by governments developing flexible community based solutions through community partnerships and supporting them with funds

---

20 Deutsche Welle News Service, 'Hopeful Kids Don't Riot, says British Youth Worker.' (undated).

and capacity building initiatives.'[21]

One area where initiatives could assist the community sector is in matters of compliance. Understandably and appropriately, not-for-profit organisations operate in an environment requiring high levels of legal and regulatory compliance, to ensure the integrity of the sector. Operating in such an environment, however, places heavy administrative demands upon program staff, which can distract from the grassroots delivery of programs. Acknowledging this, the *What Works in Community Cohesion* report proposes that:

> one suggested model is for the local council to take on responsibility for management, financial and legal aspects of large-scale voluntary or community sector initiatives (aspects where skills and experience can be weaker), freeing up project staff to focus on project delivery.[22]

Similarly, governments could provide additional attractive incentives for the business sector to partner with charitable organisations. While tax deductibility is available for financial contributions, providing attractive incentives for businesses to donate services, skills or employee hours to charities could also help build the capacity of the charitable sector. Changes in legislation to remove obstacles to philanthropic activity can promote corporate community investment and social responsibility.

Successful corporations should be championed while encouraging them to participate in philanthropic activity. Sadly, there is increasing rhetoric which condemns large corporate profits. When BHP Billiton posted a half-year profit of $10.51 billion, some were convinced this was the 'proof' that Australia needed a super-profits tax. Yet why does a company being successful mean that we should make them pay a higher percentage of tax? After all, they are already paying a higher amount of tax. Such a sentiment sounds like we are trying to encourage companies to stay mediocre by punishing them when they succeed.

I want Australian companies to be stunningly successful, and post large profits. I also want them to be exceedingly generous and give large gifts to non-profits and community organisations. These are not

---

21 The Centre for Corporate Affairs, *Corporate Community Investment in Australia*. 2007, 24-25.
22 DCLG, 2007.

necessarily mutually exclusive.

I suspect that more taxes are not the solution to alleviating poverty. Part of the solution is found in current frameworks, such as those which provide tax deductibility for giving to eligible charities. However, if government and business work together to remove hindrances, and identify incentives, more corporate investment into communities could be encouraged. If we all partner effectively, we truly can help build individuals and strengthen families.

There are many kinds of poverty in our nation, some glaringly obvious, some subtly hidden, and all of them complex in their causes and required responses. Neither government alone, nor business by itself, nor community organisations acting independently, can respond appropriately without the other. As each plays the role for which they are best suited, however, equipped and resourced by the other, families are helped and communities are strengthened.

Cindy and her daughter benefited from the way in which government, business and community organisations partnered together. These are not abstract notions. These are real people, and by working together in real ways, we all helped to put nutritious food in front of a little girl. That is a partnership we can all be proud of.

8
Fair dismissal

Grace Collier

[I]f the employee took a complaint to Fair Work Australia, there would be a first instance informal discussion. An officer of Fair Work Australia would come and meet with the employer and with the employee, and if the employer was able to show that they'd complied with the Fair Dismissal Code that they've given someone a warning, given them opportunity to improve, then the Fair Work Australia officer would say that the dismissal was fair and that there was no need for anything further.
- Julia Gillard, Deputy Prime Minister, 97.3 ABC radio, September 18 2008.

In 2009 the Australian Labor Party released a policy document called *Forward with Fairness*, its blueprint for the overhaul of workplace laws that would replace Prime Minister John Howard's 'infamous' *Work Choices Act*. In 2006, as part of *Work Choices*, businesses with fewer than 100 employees had been granted exemption from unfair dismissal legislation. This move saw unfair dismissal claims drop from 12,194 per year in the period 2005 to 2006 to 7,257 applications in the following year.

Forward with Fairness revealed plans to reverse this exemption and to broaden the coverage of the unfair dismissal legislation. The business community expressed concern. Business owners feared complicated legislation regarding rules around dismissing workers. Small business owners who were at that time exempt from the legislation were worried that the new laws would make it near impossible to dismiss staff.

In response, the then Deputy Prime Minister spoke soothingly of a simple solution, a Fair Dismissal Code.[1] This chapter examines the Code and analyses whether it has proved effective for small business people. It also examines the broadened coverage of the unfair dismissal legislation, explains the unfair dismissal process and provides real life examples of recent cases.

In addition, this chapter looks at the unfair dismissal legislation as a whole and discusses whether it adequately services the people it is supposed to service, whether there are ways to improve the employment prospects of individuals and whether the system is a good use of taxpayer funds. Consideration is given to who benefits from the current system, whether employees are treated like victims, and whether workplaces are better for the increase in a litigious mind-set. Contemplation is given to the merits of a no-fault dismissal system as an alternative method to address the needs of people after they have experienced an employment separation event.

This chapter does not address the question of unlawful dismissal, another matter altogether. Unlawful dismissal occurs where an employee, if dismissed, can take action on grounds that are prohibited by anti-discrimination legislation. For example, a person may have been sacked because they were pregnant, or gay, or of a certain race. This chapter does not propose the no-fault system replace the unlawful dismissal system.

The broadened unfair dismissal system

An employment separation event can occur in three ways. A person can resign, be dismissed or be made redundant. Under the current legislation, employees can sue their employer for unfair dismissal after any of these three paths have been taken.

This means that someone can resign their job and claim unfair dismissal. Someone can be made redundant, accept a redundancy package and claim unfair dismissal. And someone can be sacked and claim unfair dismissal. So the government has a mechanism to involve

---

1 Fair Work Australia, *Small Business Fair Dismissal Code.* July 1 2009.

itself, by making a legal judgment on and cost orders against the person whom they deem to be at fault, in every possible type of employment separation event.[2]

It should also be noted that compensation orders against persons found to be at fault for the employment separation event are almost never made against persons who are employers. Should an employee be found to be totally at fault for the employment separation, a compensation order will hardly ever be made to compensate the employer for the cost of defending the action. Persons who are eligible employees, regardless of their financial status, are considered by the system to be untouchable, while persons who are employers, regardless of their financial status, are considered by the system to be fair game.

After an employment separation event occurs, making an application for relief from an unfair dismissal is an easy online process. The applicant or their representative fills out a simple form on the Fair Work Australia website, pays a filing fee of $60 and a conference hearing is granted, usually within 28 days. Once the employee's application is lodged, regardless of the facts of the case, a conference hearing will be held.

I have assisted stunned employers who assumed that because they hold an employee resignation letter in their hand, or a redundancy letter, the conference will be cancelled. Their view has been that it is a simple matter of contacting Fair Work Australia and emailing a copy of the proof they hold to have the conference cancelled. The conference can never be cancelled, no matter what. It will be held and you are expected to attend. If you do not attend the trial a finding against you will automatically be made. Any reasons why the conference should not proceed can be made at the conference. The moment the employee's application is in the system, the 'wheel of justice' begin to roll and there is no stopping it.

A conference hearing is the first step of a two-step unfair dismissal process. A conference, often by phone, takes place between the Applicant (the ex-employee or their representative), the Respondent (the ex-employer or their representative) and a Conciliator from Fair

---

2 Those who earn above the income threshold, currently $118000 per annum, are not covered by the legislation.

Work Australia. Conferences always begin with the Conciliator running through a standard speech that, condensed and paraphrased, goes along the lines, 'Today is not about who is right and who is wrong. I will hear the parties speak but no evidence is to be put forward, as this stage is not about making judgments, it is about helping the parties settle the matter to avoid litigation.'

The Applicant is given the first chance to outline their case and then the Respondent is afforded time to speak. Because the Conciliator is not interested in making judgments they generally do not challenge claims made by either party, no matter how outlandish. They simply say things such as, 'well, if this is the case, and you can prove it at trial, then the other party may have a problem.'

The stories of the parties vary significantly and the Conciliator usually very quickly comes to the point where they say something such as, 'you are saying one thing and you are saying another, I have no idea where the truth lies. The point is that if this matter is not settled today the employer will bear the cost of an expensive trial that could cost $30000 or upwards. I am trying to assist you to avoid that situation, so as the employer, how much are you prepared to pay to settle this matter today?'

With that, the pressure upon the employer to pay 'go away money' commences. The Conciliator may point out to either party the obvious problems they could have in their case if the matter proceeds. In my experience, the Conciliator almost always places considerable pressure on the employer to settle. I have seen this pressure take many forms, including misinforming the employer about the merits of their case, pleading with them to give the employee money, or even bullying them into settling.

The process then is that the Conciliator speaks to both parties separately until a resolution (amount of money) is agreed upon. Once this is agreed, settlement documents change hands and the matter is discontinued. If, however, the parties cannot agree on an amount, Fair Work Australia issues a certificate to state that they have tried to assist but the matter was not settled. After receiving the certificate, the applicant has additional time to make an application to proceed to the second step of an unfair dismissal application.

Two examples of conference cases

Of the last five unfair dismissal applications I have defended for clients, three have been instances of employee resignation.

The two examples below both relate to employees with less than six months' service and therefore, according to legislation, exempt from the unfair dismissal system because they are within the probationary period. Such employees are only exempted from the second stage of an application, never the first stage; the conciliation conference where the Conciliator pushes to facilitate the payment of 'go away money', regardless of the merits of the case.

One case involved a real estate agent of one month's employment who unfortunately crashed his car (not while at work) and did not have insurance and so was without a car. He resigned his employment and made an application for relief from an unfair dismissal.

The conference was held in Fair Work Australia in front of a Commissioner, although the Applicant chose to attend by phone hookup. The Applicant submitted that he had resigned because he felt he had no option, because he had no car and having a car was a requirement of the job. My submission in response was simply to agree with everything the Applicant had put forward, express some sympathy for his predicament and look blankly at the Commissioner.

The Commissioner appeared very sympathetic towards the Applicant and perturbed about his predicament. The Commissioner asked me to consider a settlement of eight weeks pay to 'avoid the matter going to trial'. Over the next hour and a half significant pressure, and what I consider misinformation about the merits of the case, was given to me in the presence of my client. Towards the end of the conference, sensing my resolve against settling, the Commissioner addressed my client directly, in a pleading tone: 'look, he's really in a tight spot, you wouldn't just give him five grand would you?'

At no stage did the Commissioner inform the Applicant that he had no case, that he was within his probationary period and that he was in fact unable to proceed to the second stage of the unfair dismissal process due to legislative exemption. Instead, the Commissioner used the position and authority to attempt to assist the employee financially. Had the employer been unrepresented or represented by someone with a more compliant attitude than I, they would have conceded and made payment of settlement monies.

Another case involved a small business that had some difficulty with a young receptionist of four months' service. The employee was taking a lot of time off and the manager had discussed the matter with her. A resignation followed, followed closely by an unfair dismissal claim. The conference took place in Fair Work Australia and not by telephone. The employee's lawyer submitted the discussion with the manager had led the employee to feel 'so uncomfortable' that she had to resign. The employee had become pregnant and there was the accusation that her 'dismissal' had been due to the pregnancy.

Again, the Commissioner introduced no facts or realism into the situation, did not challenge in any way allegations that were clearly a stretch of the facts, and instead placed significant pressure on the employer (herself a pregnant young female) to settle and avoid an 'expensive trial'. Again, only my presence ensured the pressure was firmly resisted.

The conference stage of the unfair dismissal process is just a game of bluff conducted in front of an umpire who feels compelled to assist the alleged victim by enabling them to access some of the employer's money. Settlements are referred to, and measured by, the number of weeks pay rather than the dollar amount. Telling a person they should pay someone 12 weeks' pay has a lesser impact than telling them to pay someone, for example, $14,497.73

At conference, each party has a story to tell. The stories differ, and the Conciliator, who never challenges any of the Applicant's allegations, no matter how outrageous, frivolous or vexatious, dissuades both parties from proceeding to a trial. As the employer is the only one that is assumed to be in the position to make the whole thing go away by producing money, pressure is placed on the employer by the Conciliator to do so. Employers are often unrepresented or badly represented, at conference, and so, instead of, as they mostly should, staring down the threat of a trial, they produce funds to settle.

More than 95 percent of unfair dismissal cases are settled at the conference stage by employers who clearly want to avoid a trial comprising government examination and judgment as to who was at fault for an employment separation event. As at last count, according to the Fair Work Australia report to Senate estimates hearings, every working day, regardless of fairness, truth or the merits of the Applicant's case, somewhere between $80,599 and $127,805 is paid out in order to avoid the second stage of the unfair dismissal process, a full trial.

Two examples of full trial decisions

Last year, an Accountant made redundant from AP Eagers, a car dealership, pursued an unfair dismissal case right through to the full trial stage. His redundancy package was $30,000. The accountant's argument was that his employer should have offered him a junior position on a reduced pay rate, instead of making him redundant. He nominated the position he said he would have wanted; that of assistant accountant, which had a salary of more than 26 percent less than his original job. The Fair Work Commissioner agreed with him. Finding against the employer, the Commissioner said it would have been reasonable for the employee to be redeployed to lower paid duties and so awarded the accountant an extra amount of $25,000 as compensation for being unfairly dismissed.

In another case that went to full trial in 2010, a Commissioner reinstated a pilot to his former position at Regional Express Airlines, although she found he had committed misconduct. The Commissioner said the pilot's conduct which led to his dismissal 'at its best was foolish and silly from a person in the position of responsibility of a captain. At worst the conduct was wilful, may have put others in danger, and showed a scant disregard for the employer's property.' Regardless, she said the dismissal was harsh in the circumstances, given his 14 years service, seniority, and the effect of the termination because the dismissal had led to the pilot losing his income, and contributed to him having to sell his house. He had also had to pursue endorsement on other aircraft to gain employment, at a cost of $32,000.

When a government authority determines whether the process of an employment separation was correct (as well as for a justifiable reason), then the legislated remedy for failure on the employer's part is primarily reinstatement. However, reinstatement is the ultimate slap in the face for the employer and the greatest victory for a recalcitrant employee. It neuters the business owner, demoralises the management team and engenders contempt for the company in the rest of the workforce. A reinstated employee will forever onwards (and quite accurately) consider themselves 'above the law' in the workplace. Our legislative framework does not consider the impact of their likely future misconduct in the workplace upon other workers.

The Fair Dismissal Code – can small business comply?

The Small Business Fair Dismissal Code came into operation on July 1 2009. It applies to small business employers with fewer than 15 employees.

The Fair Work Australia website says:

> Small business employees cannot make a claim for unfair dismissal in the first 12 months following their engagement. If an employee is dismissed after this period and the employer has followed the Code then the dismissal will be deemed to be fair.[3]

However, employees of small business can make an application after any employment separation event and, if they do, a conciliation conference will be held. A person can work for a small business for one day, resign with no notice and put in an unfair dismissal claim, a conference will be held and the employer is advised they must attend. The website goes on to say:

> **Summary Dismissal**
>
> It is fair for an employer to dismiss an employee without notice or warning when the employer believes on reasonable grounds that the employee's conduct is sufficiently serious to justify immediate dismissal. Serious misconduct includes theft, fraud, violence and serious breaches of occupational health and safety procedures. For a dismissal to be deemed fair it is sufficient, though not essential, that an allegation of theft, fraud or violence be reported to the police. Of course, the employer must have reasonable grounds for

---

3 Fair Work Australia, 2009, 1.

making the report.[4]

Other Dismissal

In other cases, the small business employer must give the employee a reason why he or she is at risk of being dismissed. The reason must be a valid reason based on the employee's conduct or capacity to do the job. The employee must be warned verbally or preferably in writing, that he or she risks being dismissed if there is no improvement.

The small business employer must provide the employee with an opportunity to respond to the warning and give the employee a reasonable chance to rectify the problem, having regard to the employee's response. Rectifying the problem might involve the employer providing additional training and ensuring the employee knows the employer's job expectations.[5]

Procedural Matters

A small business employer will be required to provide evidence of compliance with the Code if the employee makes a claim for unfair dismissal to Fair Work Australia, including evidence that a warning has been given (except in cases of summary dismissal). Evidence may include a completed checklist, copies of written warning(s), a statement of termination or signed witness statements.[6]

In the first three quarters of the 2010-2011 financial year there were 1876 employee applications to Fair Work Australia for unfair dismissal that related to a small business. Of these, only two were struck out because Fair Work Australia found that the small business owner was able to follow the Fair Dismissal Code. These astonishing figures demonstrate that hardly anyone can comply with the Code.

Is our current system good for anyone?

The current unfair dismissal system surely must inhibit employment. The perception is that you cannot sack anyone no matter what they have

---

4 Fair Work Australia, 2009, 1.
5 Fair Work Australia, 2009, 1
6 Fair Work Australia, 2009, 2

done to anyone else. Employers are starting to realise that no one can resign, or be made redundant, without the prospect of an unfair dismissal claim. Employees routinely make unfair dismissal applications when sacked within their six-month probationary period and conferences are always held. This makes a mockery of the probationary period.

Google the words 'unfair dismissal' and look at the first advertisements that pop up. No win-no pay law firms profiting from the new system are taking advantage of the scheme and the ease with which it delivers an income. The time that goes into getting a claim to the first stage is less than three hours. In exchange for that, law firms take 50 percent on a no win-no pay basis of the 'go away' money achieved at the first stage. It is a lucrative activity feeding a burgeoning industry.

The current system places the rights of some workers over the rights of other workers. What about the workers who have to work with the person they all wish to be rid of? What about the workers who are called on to do overtime too often because their employer is too scared to hire the extra staff they need? What about all the workers who are kept on as casuals forever because the employer perceives they can sack them if they need to?

The rights of the broader workforce have diminished as the rights of the separated individual have been elevated beyond reason. Procedural nitpicking and legislative technicality has taken charge over common sense. Bureaucracy, misuse of the public service and the power it brings fails to deliver what people really need when they are just out of a job.

No-fault dismissal system

Mention the phrase 'no-fault dismissal' and most people react with abject horror. But a no-fault system does not mean that employees have no rights. It does not mean there is no support available. It does not mean that government plays no part or takes no interest in employment separation events. A no-fault system just means that no one needs to be found to be at fault for the employment separation event. It means that a whole lot of time and money is not spent pinning the blame on either the employee or the employer solely because a person no longer works in their workplace.

So what does having a no-fault dismissal system actually deliver for people? Broadly speaking, the underlying principle of the system is that any intervention by a government authority into an employment separation event must be a worthwhile intervention that provides genuine assistance to those who authentically need it. The best things you can do to help someone who has just quit or been sacked from their job is to make sure they are emotionally okay, have enough money and support and help them to find another job. The best thing is not to encourage them to engage in litigation, the associated levels of self-delusion and avoidance of reality that litigation requires and the outlook of a victim that it produces,

The first part of a no-fault system would be an employee entitlement to a notice paid period longer than currently applies. The current notice period could double or even triple and employers would happily pay it, if it meant they could dismiss without having to give a reason and without facing an unfair dismissal claim. The money employers waste on wages whilst they avoid disciplining employees would probably be greater than the cost of a long notice period. A longer notice period would need to provide sufficient disincentive to any managers inclined to sack employees randomly in a fit of pique. In this way, employees could be sure that the no-fault system does not mean a no-rights system.

The second part of the system would be a mechanism for third-party involvement for the sole purpose of providing assistance services to those employees traumatised or angry after an employment separation event. The cost of this system would probably be cheaper than what exists now. The Fair Work Australia Conciliators currently act like social workers; they may as well be social workers. They can be required to make an assessment of what led to the employment separation event and determine the present genuine needs of the employee, if any. This should not be a process that the ex-employer can be compelled to participate in. Once a person's needs are established, referrals and pathways to access appropriate services can be facilitated. Appropriate remedies for a painful separation process can include counselling to mend hurt feelings, career guidance, and support to transition into new employment opportunities.

It is my experience that the vast majority of dismissals at the employer's instigation come about due to conduct rather than performance issues on the part of the employee. Conduct issues in the workplace are what could be described as undiagnosed personality disorders, bad attitude and other behavioural problems. It is in the long-term interests of employees and the community that these issues are addressed and just after an employment separation event is the perfect time for this to occur. If undesirable conduct led to a person being sacked then the problem needs to be fixed or it will likely happen again. Here is where public money can be spent usefully to provide long-term solutions to the benefit of people, the workplace and society.

The rights in law to unfair dismissal can now be considered a property or entitlement and so perhaps employers and employees should be allowed to negotiate around those. If the government is not prepared to dismantle the system and legislate compensatory longer notice periods for all, then perhaps they will allow employees to opt out voluntarily. As part of individual flexibility arrangements, employees could waive the right to unfair dismissal for a longer notice period of dismissal or, say, a higher annual salary. Employers would pay for that. Employees who were confident in their attractiveness to and performance for an employer would benefit greatly as well. Workers, backing themselves, would have 'skin in the game'.

The move to a no-fault system entails an extension of trust in the ability of employers and employees to make arrangements between themselves. Within Labor's *Fair Work Act*, a similar trust was shown in respect to rules governing Collective Agreement making. So why not extend the confidence shown to the unfair dismissal regime?

The Labor government was the first to remove a Union Officials right to be a legal party to or sign on anyone's behalf, a Collective Agreement with an employer. Employees are the only legal party that can make an agreement with an employer and they must vote on the agreement and sign it themselves. If they so choose, then Unions can be involved at the behest of an employee but only as 'bargaining agents' with the same status and power as any other member of the public that can be nominated as a bargaining agent.[7]

The most common response to the suggestion of a no-fault system

---

7 *Fair Work Act 2009*, Part 2-4 Enterprise Agreements.

is that employers will sack at will. This argument may or may not be true, but a no-fault system would never test it because a no-fault system does not mean a no-rights system or a no-help system or a system where employers do not pay. A no-fault system means accepting that the employment relationship has been severed and that it is better to look to the future with practical assistance rather than looking to the past with judgment.

9
Foreign aid a road to hell paved with good intentions

Peter Urban

TONY JONES: Are you worried that aid, the aid budget, foreign aid in Australia, is becoming politicised?

TIM COSTELLO: Yes, I am. It goes back to Richard Nixon: "There ain't no votes in aid." The charity begins at home and the subtext is "and it ends at home". We'll just look after ourselves. And it's as if we set up a false contest of suffering, that we've got problems, floods, bushfires, so we'll just look after ourselves and forget our moral duties to the 1.4 billion in poverty, forget that we've made extraordinary progress. In 1960, 60,000 kids died each day. We halved that to 30000 kids dying each day just two years ago. It's down now to 22000 children dying each day. A lot of that's actually due to very simple aid interventions - rehydration kits for kids with diarrhoea, which is the biggest killer, mosquito nets, vitamin supplements. We are saving lives, and when Australians hear that, I think they start to gain confidence in what we're doing.[1]

A brief history of aid

In foreign aid it is a truism that the road to hell is filled with good intentions. The intentions of foreign aid are good – to alleviate poverty. And the countries in which foreign aid operates are, in many cases, hell on earth. But foreign aid is not about intentions; it is, or should be, about outcomes.

Since World War II, international development assistance (foreign aid) can be divided into two stages. From 1945 to about 1965, aid

---

1 Australian Broadcasting Corporation, *Lateline*. April 14 2011.

was dominated by post-war reconstruction assistance. Since 1965 to the present, however, aid has widened its scope, country coverage and the amount of aid involved (in dollar terms) quite substantially. However, this expansion in aid has not been matched by commensurate outcomes.

Australian aid is a child of the second stage. In 2011-12, Australia's aid program will provide $4.8 billion in official development assistance. Not a lot of money when expressed as a proportion of GDP – less than 0.5 percent. But it is a lot of money in dollar terms, and in terms of what Australia could achieve to reduce poverty at home.

In economic terms, this is the opportunity cost of our aid program. In absolute terms, poverty and the need for aid may be greater overseas, but the simple fact is (despite what Tim Costello tries to tell us), in assessing aid, charity really does begin at home. Fiscal resources are finite. As a result, governments have to make tough choices about where and how they use these resources. When it comes to reducing poverty, more is known about poverty in Australia. It is closer and hence cheaper to address, and easier to manage and to monitor.

This point is important. Decisions about aid have to balance the need for aid with the costs and risks in delivering the aid. If the costs and risks of foreign aid are high, then Australia is probably better off using the aid funds to reduce poverty at home.

To understand how well Australian aid policy has done in terms of outcomes, the objective of aid policy has to be understood. The usual goal of aid and the one used by the Australian Agency for International Development (AusAID) is to alleviate poverty. For aid policy, however, the goal is to lift large numbers of people out of poverty.

Why the distinction? Essentially it is about causes and costs.

If the goal of aid policy is simply to lift people out of poverty, then aid could be left to non-government organisations (NGOs), and many of the costs of delivering aid could be saved. While aid is an expensive business even for NGOs, for governments the costs are greater as governmentally delivered aid typically involves additional layers of checks and balances to ensure transparency and to demonstrate effectiveness.

When we talk about aid policy, however, we are not focusing on isolated pockets of poverty. We are focusing, instead, on reducing structural poverty. And rather than working with the poor, the strategy for aid policy also has to be to work with government in the aid recipient countries to develop better policies and governance within these countries. That is, to change the policy framework and correct the policy failures that are the cause of broad-based poverty.

When framed in this way, aid policy is conceptually fairly simple. It is about opening markets and establishing property rights and addressing public goods and externalities such as health, education and research, particularly agricultural research. This collection of policies has commonly been referred to as the 'Washington consensus'. This simple aid model has worked. The great aid success stories, West Germany and Western Europe (through the Marshall Plan), Japan and South Korea are all poster children for this market-based aid model.

Unfortunately, these aid policy successes seem to have become the exceptions. In the two decades up to the early 2000s, despite its growth, aid seems to have lost its way.

The reasons were fourfold. Most obviously, aid in most of the early positive examples was driven by the United States. As with free trade, history will show that successful aid needs a champion. In the reconstruction stage, the United States was a vigorous champion.

The second factor was social and political cohesion in the recipient countries. The devastation of war can unite a country behind recovery, but it was more than simply social unity. There was also political cohesion in the first four of the poster children for the market model.

The third factor was focus. Aid was first and foremost about getting the economies in question functioning well after the devastation of war. Of course, the US had an ulterior motive – this was the period of the Cold War – but the aid was in the spirit of President John Fitzgerald Kennedy's 1963 statement of solidarity with West Berlin.

The reform process also exhibited scale. The aid program was broadly based (that is, it covered the economy as a whole, or a major part of it). It also involved substantial resources.

China and India are also more recent examples of the successful market model. In both China and India, the catalyst for policy reform was domestic politics, not aid, and the policy goal was to lift per capita economic growth. The approach adopted nevertheless reflected the key features of the earlier aid successes: market-oriented policy reforms, scale (the policy reforms were broad based), and they had a clear focus (faster GDP growth).

More recently, however, aid policy typically appears to have three objectives:

- aid in the narrow sense of poverty alleviation
- security/defence, and
- trade.

In a sense, the multiple objectives provide some justification for the expansion of aid programs. These multiple objectives for aid, however, are often in conflict.

Take, for example, security. Australia often provides aid assistance to governments or, more accurately, regimes that we would not deal with in normal circumstances. Because of governance problems, these aid programs deliver poor outcomes or fail. Worse, the aid can often further fragment and destroy the social cohesion necessary for aid success. It also has a second impact through failed accountability. Because of the conflicting objectives, poor aid outcomes are accepted as a small price for greater security. Indeed, the reality is that both the aid and the security objectives are not met. The same holds for trade. The history of the aid program is littered with industry assistance (not trade) projects dressed up as aid.

When I began my research for this paper, in June 2011, I had hoped that trade projects dressed up as aid (a common feature of Australian aid in the 1990s) had become the exception rather than the norm, but the recent animal cruelty scandal involving live cattle exports to Indonesia suggests otherwise. However, there were still frequent livestock industry demands that the Australian government should be using aid funds to improve slaughter practices in Indonesian abattoirs with deficient practices. Such aid spending would do little to reduce Indonesian poverty. If the Australian cattle industry wants the benefits of sales to the Indonesian market, they should pay for it directly, not seek to pass the cost to the aid program. Aid policies that alleviate poverty in Indonesia will in time benefit the Australian cattle industry, but the focus of the policies should be aid, not industry assistance dressed up as aid.

This point applies to any industry, including defence (and security more generally). Good aid will usually be good for trade and good for security, but defence/security policies dressed up as aid rarely do much to reduce poverty.

The current aid program

There is a prima facie case that the current aid program needs to be reconsidered and replaced by an alternative aid strategy based on social justice. For example, a 2003 review of aid policy concluded:

> Australia's aid programme is significant, particularly in the Pacific, totaling (in 2000-01 terms) around $50 billion since 1975. It also accounts for a significant and growing share of scarce national savings. Despite this, our aid programme has been a dismal failure.[2]

Since then, AusAID has made one step forward and one step back. The step forward is a good one. AusAID now has a fairly clear goal to alleviate poverty. The actual objective of the aid program is 'to assist developing countries to reduce poverty and achieve sustainable development, in line with Australia's national interest'. Fairly clear because, as the recent review of aid effectiveness notes, the phrase 'in line with Australia's national interest' is not at all clear.

The step backwards is a sad one. Until recently, Australian aid was heavily focused on the western Pacific. It is now all over the place – quite literally. As noted earlier, to be successful aid has to be focused. It would appear that Australia's aid strategy has lost its focus. Australian aid is spread around a great deal (see Figure 1).

Worse, a lot of Australian aid is not really aid. In Iraq, for example, aid money is used to clean up our own mess as well as that of others, caused in the largely fruitless search for WMD. A similar situation applies in Afghanistan, where large aid sums are also being spent, with similar likely questionable prospects for positive long-term poverty reduction outcomes.

---

2 Peter J Urban, 'Australian Aid Policy: A Case of Lose/Lose, not Win/Win.' *Institute of Public Affairs Backgrounder.* 15(4), 2003.

Figure 1. AusAID spending by region 2010-2011

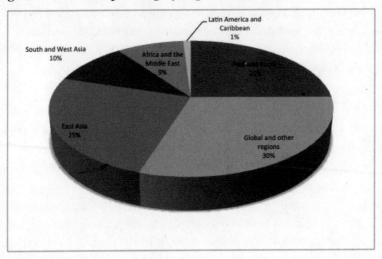

Source: AusAid, *Annual Report 2010-11*. 2011, 18.

A second major problem with our aid program is lack of detailed cost/
benefit assessments of its performance. With more than forty years of
aid delivery through AusAID and its predecessors, it should be possible
by referring to detailed official assessments to evaluate Australia's aid
performance. Unfortunately, even after all this time, there are virtually
no detailed performance assessments available.

There are, by contrast, quite a few opinion-based qualitative
assessments; evidence-based assessments are rare. In fact, the Office of
Development Evaluation (ODE) within AusAID was only established
in 2006 (despite a recommendation in the 1997 Simons Report calling
for independent external performance evaluations of aid).[3] The Office
has only published three annual evaluation reports. In its 2009 report,
the latest available, ODE stated:

> The Australian aid program has made a great deal of progress in
> terms of monitoring the performance of its *inputs* [my emphasis],
> however, progress in supporting the monitoring and evaluation

---

3 Simons Report, 'The Australian Overseas Aid Program: One Clear Objective Poverty
Reduction Through Sustainable Development.' *Report of the Committee of Review*. April 1997.

systems of partner countries has not always been as great. There has been a tendency to develop complex systems for tracking the progress of individual (donor-supported) projects, rather than systems for monitoring key performance indicators and carrying out joint analysis with partner countries. Such systems do little to support policymaking and budgeting on a national scale.[4]

This state of affairs would be unsatisfactory for any government expenditure program, but it is of extremely serious concern given that the Australian government has spent more than $100 billion on aid (in 2010-11 terms) during the last four decades. Unless the lack of proper economic evaluation reflects a fear that detailed performance evaluation would show that the aid spending has produced little in terms of value for money, the lack of detailed formal assessments is otherwise inexplicable. Instead, simplistic performance indicators have to be relied upon to answer the question about aid effectiveness.

Fortunately, the major recipients of AusAID funding have done better during the last five years in terms of per capita GDP growth (see Table 1) compared to their performance from 1990 to 2001. China and India stand out, but so do PNG, East Timor and Indonesia. The question is whether there is any relationship between AusAID funding and the improved GDP growth in these countries.

Take the example of Papua New Guinea. As can be seen, per capita GDP growth more than doubled between the two periods. Much of this is the result of higher commodity prices in recent years (particularly for gold and crude oil). During the same period the local currency (kina) has appreciated, both in nominal and real terms. The only apparent blemishes in its economic performance in recent years are that PNG's current account has deteriorated sharply from a surplus of 10 percent of GDP in 2008 to a deficit of nearly 24 percent in 2010 and an even larger projected deficit in 2011, and acceleration in price inflation. PNG is verging on a failed state.

A similar story holds in many of Australia's other major aid partners such as East Timor: stronger growth (often the result of higher commodity prices), real exchange rate appreciation (particularly against the US

---

4 AusAid, *Annual Review of Development Effectiveness 2009*. December 2010.

dollar) but deterioration in their external accounts (in some cases, quite precipitous deterioration). That is the good news. The better news is that many aid recipients appear to be trying to transform their terms of trade good fortune into sustainable economic growth.

PNG is a good example of this. There, the very large current account deficit reflects investment associated with an LNG project (which is valued at more than 150 percent of GDP). When completed, this project will deliver a stream of exports that should help sustain economic growth for decades to come.

Table 1. GDP growth per capita in Australia's Top Ten Aid Recipients (1990-2001 and 2005-2010)

Aid Recipient	GDP Growth Per Capita (%)	
	1990-2001	2005-2010
Papua New Guinea	1.1	11.4
Indonesia	2.2	6.0
East Timor	4.7	8.0
Vietnam	5.8	6.8
Philippines	1.0	4.3
China	8.8	11.1
Cambodia	2.2	6.0
Solomon Islands	-11.5*	4.6
Bangladesh	2.8	6.1
India	4.0	11.2

Source: Department of Foreign Affairs and Trade.*2000-01 only.

The bad news is that this improved economic performance in aid recipients is not the product of Australia's aid. It is the result of good fortune in the form of higher commodity prices and pressure and good advice from the International Monetary Fund (IMF).

The best example of the role of the IMF for our aid recipients is India. As noted by Lal, the creation of a rent-seeking society (or 'licence Raj') gradually led to a fiscal crisis and effective bankruptcy in 1991.[5] Spurred by the IMF, a new Indian government under Manmohan Singh

---

5 D. Lal, 'An Indian Economic Miracle?' *Cato Journal.* Volume 28(1), 2008.

began a broad-ranging program of economic reforms. GDP growth accelerated from four percent to more than eight percent. Best of all, the percentage of the population living in poverty has fallen sharply since 1991. During this period, aid received by India fell significantly.

The success of the IMF in countries such as PNG, when for decades our aid failed to have much impact, should not really come as a surprise. In most countries, and not only developing countries, broad-based reforms are politically difficult to implement, with powerful interests often supporting the status quo.

Difficult reforms are usually only undertaken when the situation becomes desperate. In these situations, the IMF can often 'force' governments to accept reforms that they would otherwise either reject or try to defer.

A new aid objective and a new aid strategy

These observations of Australia's aid program have three important implications for aid policy. First, and most importantly, poverty reduction in the broader sense should be left to the IMF. This does not mean abdicating this responsibility altogether to the IMF. In many ways, it means quite the reverse.

Australia has played, and can continue to play, an important part *through* the IMF. For example, Australia usually provides the IMF Managing Director for Oceania. By doing so, it is responsible for keeping a strong IMF focus on the countries that matter to Australia in an economic development and poverty reduction sense. And Australia will need to keep this focus. As noted, higher commodity prices have contributed to the better recent economic performance in many of Australia's aid recipients. While the outlook for commodity prices is positive, the reality is that just as commodity prices have risen in recent years, they could easily fall. And given the importance of commodity exports to these countries, the economic impact would be severe – possibly requiring assistance from the IMF.

By operating through the IMF, Australia's aid program is freed of a major handicap. Bilateral relations between the IMF and individual countries seeking IMF support are sometimes tense. This is in the nature of these relationships – the countries usually find implementing IMF policy prescriptions politically painful. They only accept the pain out of necessity – the IMF is the 'lender of last resort'.

Unfortunately, major aid recipients do not see Australia in the same way as they view the IMF and, hence, they have resisted IMF-style conditionality when applied to Australian aid. It can also be politically difficult within Australia to apply tough aid conditionality. The result – the will to implement important but contentious governance and other reforms in the recipient can be weakened or lost. As a result, these policy goals should not be pursued through bilateral aid.

Rather than AusAID managing the aid program, responsibility for aid policy and reporting should be transferred to the Treasury. Treasury is already responsible for the IMF and other major multilateral development institutions such as the World Bank. As a result, there would be little change from the status quo, although the aid assessment and reporting capacity in the relevant areas of the Treasury would need to be upgraded.[6]

Second, along with the transfer of the poverty goal to the IMF, defence, security and trade goals should be pursued directly and not confounded with aid. The transfer of the poverty goal to the IMF would lead to this anyway, but there should be an explicit decision to separate defence, security and trade goals from aid and, this should be included in a formal statement of the objectives of aid policy.

Finally, there should be a refocusing of the existing bilateral aid (referred to as 'country aid' within AusAid) away from poverty and to social justice. This would involve narrowing the scope of country aid to five sectors only:

- education
- food (or agriculture)
- infrastructure (including water and basic housing)
- the environment, and
- health, humanitarian and refugee aid.

Why these five sectors? First, social justice as a concept has a number

---

6 This would also reinforce the message that aid policy is no longer really about foreign, trade or defence objectives, but about improving economic outcomes in the countries receiving Australian aid.

of interpretations. At their heart, however, all focus on the individual and access to adequate sustenance (food), housing and water; to live within a sustainable environment; and to have access to health care. These are captured by the five sectors. Second, these five sectors are covered already in the aid program and Australia has experience working in them. Australia is also very capable with sectors such as agriculture.

Because the proposed strategic shift is quite a marked departure from the current aid policy, and the strategy outlined in the report of the Independent Review of Aid Effectiveness,[7] it would be necessary to define appropriate standards for each of the five sectors and how access would be managed. This could be done, for example, through community discussions hosted by AusAID.

For the consultations, AusAID would need to prepare a background paper on the available budget (net of multilateral aid funding, which would instead be transferred to Treasury), costings for pursuing the alternative minimal social justice goals in the five nominated sectors. On the question of funding for social justice, the proposed changes in the aid strategy are not explicitly about the level of aid funding. They are about how the aid program is managed, and its focus.

In 2010-11, estimated aid spending was $4.3 billion. Of this, approximately 40 percent was spent on multilateral aid. Based on these figures, the proposed social justice program would have an estimated budget of around $2.3 billion. The AusAID background paper could use this amount as an indicative budget of $2 billion for the discussions. For the background paper, AusAID would also set out (in simple terms) an indication of the opportunity costs of this aid by, for example, illustrating what could be achieved in Australia in terms of expanded access to these five sectors for Australians living in poverty.

By limiting access to those in poverty and operating within the existing budget envelope, the proposed aid strategy should be welfare enhancing – it should make those living in poverty in the recipient countries better off without making anyone worse off. Whether, and

---

7 Commonwealth of Australia, *Independent Review of Aid Effectiveness*. 2011. While the report is good in parts, it is neither independent nor really a review of aid effectiveness. Even so, the report is critical of AusAID's evaluation of aid effectiveness (see Appendix 1, for the report's conclusions on AusAID effectiveness management).

how well, it will work in practice, only time and detailed evaluation will tell. But given the lack of detailed evaluation of aid to date, it is reasonable to assume it will not do any worse than continuing with the existing aid strategy. Moreover, the proposed social justice approach to aid should simplify the evaluation process.

Appendix 1. Managing for results and enhancing transparency, scrutiny and community engagement.[8]

The measurement of effectiveness is unquestionably harder in aid than in many businesses due to complexity of objectives and wide range of potential delivery mechanisms.

Over the past five years, AusAID has invested heavily in performance management and increased the focus on results.

AusAID, and to some extent the broader aid program, is also subject to a variety of external performance reviews, from Australian National Audit Office (ANAO) reports, peer reviews by the OECD Development Assistance Committee (DAC), parliamentary oversight and government–commissioned reviews.

The ANAO and OECD DAC have positively assessed AusAID's system of self–rating projects, which puts AusAID at the forefront of bilateral donors. However, the evaluation dimension (relating to in–depth assessments rather than across–the–board monitoring) of AusAID's performance management and reporting system is not working well. There is low compliance in relation to existing guidelines for independent evaluation reports, and little use of them to inform decision–making.

The creation in 2006 of the Office of Development Effectiveness and its Annual Review of Development Effectiveness (ARDE) were no doubt important initiatives that have helped prioritise aid effectiveness. No other bilateral donor has an equivalent to the ARDE. Overall, however, the ARDE has been a limited success, being released with increasing delay.

The Review Panel proposes that the Office of Development Effectiveness remain within AusAID, but change its name to the Office of Aid Effectiveness and focus more on evaluation. It would be responsible for undertaking and publishing each year a manageable number (say, 10–20) of high quality evaluations. The Office would also publish an annual synthesis of evaluations and a quality assurance assessment of the aid program's performance management system.

A small Independent Evaluation Committee should be appointed

---

8 C of A, 2011, 31-2.

(with both AusAID staff and several external members, including the Chair). All draft independent evaluations and the new annual synthesis report would be discussed, and then cleared, by the Independent Evaluation Committee (not AusAID), and then published.

At present, other Australian government departments, with the exception of the Australian Federal Police, do not generally apply the effectiveness measurement and reporting systems AusAID uses. In the future, all departments that spend ODA should fully participate in the aid measurement and effectiveness reporting system.

AusAID and other government agencies should adopt a single and consistent approach to measuring effectiveness. This should be based on a three–tier system with a simple 'traffic light' system rating performance against indicators in each tier:

1. progress against development goals
2. the contribution of Australian aid
3. operational and organisational effectiveness.

The Review Panel recommends that there should be an annual assessment of aid effectiveness that covers all ODA and serves two purposes: public accountability and informing the annual review and budget process. The annual assessment should include a summary scorecard using the three–tier system supported by reports on the effectiveness of major country and other programs. The annual assessment should replace the ARDE, which would be discontinued.

The net effect of the Review Panel's proposals will be a streamlined process for growing the aid program in a responsible and effective fashion.

10
Personal responsibility in preventing disease and injury

Terry Barnes

We are killing people by not acting.
- The Hon Nicola Roxon MP, then Commonwealth Minister
for Health and Ageing, launching the report of the National
Preventative Health Taskforce, October 2009.

Prevention of illness and injury as a health policy goal

Preventing illness and injury is far better and cheaper than cure. Indeed, this is one of few points of health policy consensus between Australia's progressive Left and the liberal-conservative Right. Healthy people make relatively small demands on expensive health resources in contrast to the chronically ill and frail. Those who keep themselves well for as long as possible in life are pearls beyond price.

In the second decade of the 21st century, what these risks are and how we can avoid them are very well known. But, as a 2010 survey of a cross-section of American employees showed, people know how to maintain or improve their health, but many are not taking action to do much about them.[1] While there is no current comparable Australian survey data, the continuing prevalence of lifestyle-related health problems in Australia suggests that current policy settings are not working.

By far the greatest effort has gone into confronting causal factors

---

[1] National Business Group on Health/Hewitt Associates, *The Employee Mindset: Views, Behaviors and Solutions.* 2010, 3-8.

that a preponderance of scientific and clinical evidence are most directly influenced by individuals' lifestyles and personal behaviour: tobacco use (including lung cancer, respiratory and circulatory problems); excessive consumption of alcohol (including liver damage, pancreatitis, cardiac disease, cancer, mental illness and attributable social problems and injury risks); and excessive calorie consumption and under-exercising (including obesity, nutrition problems, diabetes, musculoskeletal problems, coronary disease and kidney failure).

A common measure of the value of prevention is burden of disease, which attempts to quantify the personal, social and economic impacts of acute and chronic illness and injury. A major 2008 burden of disease study by the Australian Institute of Health and Welfare (AIHW), looking at projected long-term costs of health and residential aged care, projected that:

- Overall health and related expenditure will increase by 189 percent in the period 2003-33, from $85 billion to $246 billion (in 2010-11 just over $100 billion)
- The health and aged care share of Australia's Gross Domestic product will increase from 9.3 percent in 2002-03 to 12.4 percent in 2032-33
- Spending will grow at a greater rate than if simply due to natural population and demographic-related demand growth because of so-called conditions with preventable causes such as diabetes, cardiovascular and musculoskeletal diseases, and
- There will also be significant growth in high treatment cost areas including cancer, mental disorders and, above all, dementia.[2]

Such projections are like Dickens' Ghost of Christmas Yet to Come: they show the *shadows* of what may be, rather than what definitely will be. As yet unknown research and treatment breakthroughs, new technology and emerging demographic and behavioural trends can either confirm or confound such forecasts. Nevertheless, such stark

---

2 Australian Institute of Health and Welfare, *Projections of Australian Health Care Expenditure by Disease*. Canberra, December 2008, Executive Summary and Chapter 3.

estimates remind us that a considerable proportion of health outlays would not be needed at all if it were not for individual lifestyles and choices.

Social justice and access to health care

Former Health Minister Nicola Roxon's comment on the National Preventative Health Taskforce report, opening this chapter, assumes blithely that government has a duty to intervene in people's lives, presumably for their own good. Prevention-related policy is cast almost entirely in terms of the state's duty to protect its citizens from harm rather than assuming that each person has a responsibility to protect her or himself.

Most policy-makers, opinion-leaders, health professionals and pressure groups, forming what can be termed the Australian health establishment, share this view. It also dominates the policy agendas of Australian governments – federal, state, conservative, progressive. But there is a pragmatic, alternate conception of social justice that challenges this activist approach, summed up by the British cabinet minister, former Conservative leader and founder of the Centre for Social Justice, Iain Duncan Smith: 'The public ... defined it [social justice], profoundly, as 'help for those who genuinely need help, and help for those who deliver that help.'[3]

Arguably, there is a third strand to Duncan Smith's practical definition: *above all, help for those who help themselves*. This third element is conspicuous by its absence in topical discourse on mitigating risks to the good health of both individuals and their communities. This chapter considers the status quo and whether introducing the signature Australian social policy innovation of mutual obligation into healthcare can challenge it.

The health gospel according to Marmot

Between 2005 and 2010 two major policy projects dazzled the great and good of the health world. The first was the work of the World

---

3 I. Duncan Smith, 'Families, Poverty and Social Justice, a UK Perspective.' *Speech to the Institute of Marriage and Family*, Ottawa, March 12 2009.

Health Organisation's (WHO) Commission on Social Determinants of Health, which reported in 2008. The second was a policy review commissioned by the British government in response to the WHO study, which reported in late 2010.

The common thread is that both were led by British (and partly Australian-trained) professor of public health and epidemiology, Sir Michael Marmot, who has become to public health policy what his countryman Lord Stern is to climate change – a global (and globetrotting) figurehead of an activist policy movement. Between them, Marmot's two reviews reached the fundamental conclusions that inequalities in personal health status are overwhelmingly due to social factors. As the British review put it: 'There is a social gradient in health – the lower a person's social position, the worse his or her health.'[4]

Marmot advocates massive and whole-of-government actions to address identified inequalities and what are commonly called the 'social determinants of health' – inferior living conditions, social status, education and income. His response is summed up succinctly in three 'overarching recommendations' in his WHO commission report:

- Improve daily living conditions
- Tackle the inequitable distribution of money, power and resources, and
- Measure and understand the problem and assess the impact of action.[5]

Marmot fails to recognise that individuals and their choices can shape or influence their own health status and experiences. Indeed, a textual search in both his reports for the words 'personal responsibility' is fruitless.

In Australia, Marmot's influence is very clear in the report in 2009 of the National Preventative Health Taskforce.[6] The Taskforce's experts advocated a comprehensive 'road map' to make Australia the healthiest

---

4 Strategic Review of Health Inequalities in England post-2010, *Fair Society, Healthy Lives* (*The Marmot Review*). 2010, 15.
5 WHO Commission on the Social Determinants of Health, *Closing the Gap in A Generation: Health Equity through Addressing the Social Determinants of Health*. 2008, 2.
6 National Preventative Health Taskforce, *Australia: The Healthiest Country by 2020*. Canberra 2009.

nation by 2020, a goal adopted with little question by the Rudd and Gillard governments. The Taskforce's detailed prescription reflected the Marmot orthodoxy that poorer and implicitly ignorant people need protection from bad nutrition, smoking and drinking too much. It embraced supply-side deterrent penalties, notably higher taxes on cigarettes and alcohol to put these beyond easy reach of the less well-off on the assumption that these are affordable, if guilty, pleasures.[7]

Marmot and the Australian Health Establishment's message is simple: poor but avoidable personal health outcomes are not individuals' faults. Rather, they are the result of social, economic and educational disadvantage, and political powerlessness.[8] In this taxonomy, avoidable illness and injury flow from self-serving marketing and media manipulation by, particularly, Big Tobacco, Big Alcohol, Big Gambling and Big Advertising. Unsurprisingly, the proposed counter to this 'axis of evil' is heavy intervention by the biggest of them all – Big Government.

Indeed, health elites take a dim view of the capacity of ordinary Australians to make reasoned judgments about what is good and bad for them.[9] This paternalist attitude is well-illustrated by government and interest group advocacy over plain cigarette packaging: the implicit policy case that consenting adults are wooed to bright shiny images and marketing like small children.[10] It is also a feature in the case for mandatory pre-commitment for gaming machine gamblers.[11]

---

7 Searching the Taskforce's report for the words 'personal responsibility' is a waste of time.

8 Laverty and Callaghan's book, *Determining the Future: A Fair Go and Health for All*, 2011 illustrates the *zeitgeist*. It draws together opinion-formers to Australianise the Marmot health inequality thesis with the aim of adopting Marmot's recommendations in Australia.

9 This is reminiscent of Aristotle's dichotomy of natural masters and servants in *The Politics*, where he wrote: *That some should rule, and others be ruled is a thing, not only necessary, but expedient; from the hour of their birth, some are marked out for subjection, others for rule*. Aristotle, *The Politics*. Book I.

10 For example, Becky Freeman, Simon Chapman and Matthew Rimmer, *The Case for the Plain Packaging of Tobacco Products*. The University of Sydney, School of Public Health, 2007.

11 For example, The Rev Tim Costello, 'The Game's Up – Pokies Reform not so Taxing for Footy.' *The Age*. September 27 2011.

Health care and perverse behaviour

Armed with reliable knowledge we all can preserve our health, either by avoiding a risky activity (such as giving up smoking or not starting at all), or mitigate risk (such as reducing the number of cigarettes smoked, or their tar and nicotine content).

But there will always be those who ignore the warning signs and messages and choose to plunge headlong down the road to personal perdition, or simply are apathetic about their health. Nevertheless, in prevailing Marmotian policy orthodoxy the reckless, feckless, cupid and stupid are not held responsible for the consequences of their own behaviour – there is always someone else to blame.

In Australia, universal and unconditional access to publicly-subsidised medical and public hospital services is a de facto right. Further, publicly-subsidised private health insurance is 'community rated': that is, the community of *insured persons*, which tends by its nature to be generally older and/or disproportionately carrying significant risks of needing treatment than the general population. By law, no-one is turned away from private health insurance on grounds of age or known risk, and everyone pays the same premiums for the same cover, whether they are in the peak of fitness and health, chronically ill or frail aged.[12]

Two widely-reported international cases illustrate instances of perverse behaviour that in Australia would have taxpayer-subsidised access to Medicare, free public hospital treatment and, if they chose, community-rated private health insurance.

Case 1

In 1993 a middle-aged man, Harry Elphick, was admitted to a Manchester hospital with heart problems. His doctors asked him to quit his 25-cigarette daily habit before undergoing major surgery. Elphick initially refused. He subsequently relented, but died before surgery could be done. His widow said later: 'It shouldn't have mattered whether he smoked or not, he should have been given treatment. It is wrong and quite

---

12 The Howard Government introduced the most recent legislative changes to private health insurance legislation in 2006-07, and the most strenuous opposition to changes reducing regulation on what health funds can cover came from the health bureaucracy itself.

disgusting.' Few disagreed, and Elphick's surgeon was demonised for confronting Elphick, even though Elphick himself had ignored all warnings. 'This is not a moral view, simply pragmatic,' the surgeon responded, noting it was in the clear interests of patients to give up smoking before surgery.[13]

David Blunkett, then the British Labour Party's health spokesman, harrumphed: 'Everyone has a right to access to the National Health Service, no matter how foolish they have been in their own behaviour, whether that is in smoking or in fooling about in a boxing ring or on a rugby pitch', he said. 'A doctor's role is to heal and not to judge,' *The Independent* newspaper editorialised.[14]

Case 2

In 2010 and 2011 world media covered an American woman, Donna Simpson, whose sole ambition is to eat her way into the Guinness Book of Records as the world's most obese woman, with a personal goal of weighing 1000 pounds (455 kilograms).[15] Simpson already was the world's fattest woman to give birth, in a complex caesarean in 2007 that required a medical team of 30. At that time she was almost 80 kilograms lighter than her weight in 2011. She derives income through her website, charging voyeuristic viewers to watch her eat.[16]

Barely walking and suffering high blood pressure, heart disease and diabetes, Simpson is unemployed, a single mother and socially isolated. The financial costs of her fecklessness are not hers, but passed on to taxpayers who will have to cover the medical and support costs of her morbid obesity under the Medicaid scheme, including diabetic and cardiovascular complications, as well as the collateral costs of social services for an unemployable and

---

13 'Death of Briton Denied Operation Fires Health Care Debate.' *The New York Times*. August 21 1993.
14 'The Fag-End of Medical Care.' *The Independent*. August 18 1993.
15 'Mother Aiming to be World's Fattest Woman Earns $90K a Year from Fans Who Watch Her Eating Online.' *Daily Mail*. July 14 2011.
16 www.officialdonnasimpson.com

housebound individual.

In 1963, Harvard economist, Kenneth Arrow, wrote famously about moral hazard applying to clinical choices by doctors spending the money of third-party payers instead of their patient's.[17] But where generous public and private healthcare subsidies exist, cases like these highlight that the parallel problem of *patient* moral hazard – the reckless, feckless, cupid and stupid assuming taxpayers or other health insurance policy-holders will pick up the tab for their bad choices.

If living in Australia, both Elphick and Simpson would know that if they needed expensive treatment as a result of their voluntarily-assumed risks, they have recourse to Medicare, the Pharmaceutical Benefits Scheme, free public patient cover in public hospitals and access to community-rated private health insurance to spread their assumed risks over their fellow insured persons. Our system's universality is a perverse incentive for recklessness, fecklessness, cupidity and stupidity.

Sticks and carrots – trends in American employee health plans

The problematic relationship between insurance and moral hazard has become a significant issue in the United States, where employers pay health insurance premiums for the majority of working Americans and their families. Motivated by two driving factors, premium costs and concern for the overall health and productivity of their employees, employers increasingly are moving to give their staff cash and non-cash incentives to participate in health risk assessments, health improvement programs and to improve their management of chronic conditions. But they also are moving increasingly to incorporate penalties for poor behaviours and poor compliance with health improvement plans.

A health trends survey in 2010 by US consultancy Hewitt Associates looked at the take-up rates of employer of specific carrot and stick measures for staff and insured dependants in 2009 and 2010:[18]

17 K. Arrow, 'Uncertainty and the Welfare Economics of Medical Care.' *The American Economic Review*. December 1963, 941-73.
18 Hewitt Associates, *The Road Ahead: Under Construction with Increasing Tolls*. 2010, especially 13-18. In December 2009-January 2010 Hewitt surveyed nearly 600 individual employer-provided health benefit programmes covering roughly 10 million employees and dependants. About 350 of the surveyed companies were among the US's largest employers.

Carrots

Companies offering cash incentives for participating in:	% in 2009	% in 2010
Health risk assessment questionnaire	35	63
Health improvement/wellness programmes	29	37
Disease management programmes	14	17

Sticks

Hewitt found that, in 2010, 47 percent of surveyed companies were planning to impose penalties or disincentives for non-participation in certain health improvement activities over the next three years, with 18 percent of companies surveyed already doing so:[19]

Employee health plans involving penalties: Penalties for specific unhealthy behaviours or non-compliance in health management programmes	%
Smoker surcharge	64
Require participation with disease management/lifestyle behaviour programmes or pay a penalty	50
Require biometric screening (eg blood pressure, Body Mass Index measurement) or pay a penalty	45
Require participation with health coach or pay a penalty	25
Require biometric improvements (eg lower blood pressure, BMI) or pay a penalty	17

Hewitt also found that the commonest penalty preferred by employers was increasing employees' shares of health insurance premiums. Higher deductions, out-of-pockets and co-payments were also identified as sticks.[20] Nevertheless, imposing penalties as well as offering incentives is controversial in the US. Some argue that it is ethically fraught and

---

19 Hewitt Associates, 2010, 18.
20 Hewitt Associates, 2010, 18.

discriminates against the weak, the predisposed and the poor.[21]
But it is working and popular. Could it work in Australia?

Moving towards mutual obligation healthcare in Australia

An Australian individual-responsibility approach to healthcare could require some sort of 'mutual obligation contract', under which a person is assisted in return for pursuing positive health behaviours.

Adapting Pearson and Lieber's suggested principles for applying penalties in American employee health plans,[22] promoting individual responsibility through carrots and sticks would ensure that:

- Australians have reasonable access to reliable, balanced, evidence-based and easily-understood information about avoidable health conditions, such as diabetes and obesity, and that related health risks can be avoided or mitigated by individuals
- Public and private investment ensures sufficient health improvement, risk minimisation and chronic condition management services to support individuals at risk
- Individuals are in no doubt the penalty risks they run if they do not fulfil their side of the mutual obligation contract
- Individuals are given reasonable notice to shape up, and reasonable time to make an effort to turn things around before any rewards or penalties are applied
- Illness, injuries and inherited conditions beyond a person's control are not held against them
- Mutual obligation in healthcare applies without regard to a person's social, ethnic or economic status, and
- Individuals' reasonable capacity to pay (now or in the future) should be taken into account, while not being used as an excuse to avoid penalties.

---

21 See, for example, C. Andre, M. Velasquez and T. Mazur, 'Voluntary Health Risks: Who Should Pay?' *Responsive Community*. Spring 1994, 73-77.
22 S. Pearson and S. Lieber, 'Financial Penalties for the Unhealthy? Ethical Guidelines for Holding Employees Responsible for Their Health.' *Health Affairs*. May/June 2009, 845-52.

Rewarding good behaviour

The case for public and private health insurers rewarding for good risk modifying behaviour is straightforward. For example, if somebody quits smoking, adopts a good nutrition and exercise plan, reins in their drinking or other risky behaviours, enrols and perseveres in health management or coaching programs, or simply works hard at reducing their risk profile and improving their long-term health, give them something of value in return.

Private health insurance

For privately-insured persons, rewards could be discounts on premiums, no-claim bonuses or waiver of policy excesses or waiting times, or other forms of tangible benefit such as cash payments, personal gifts or even shares in the company. The Commonwealth Government should remove any statutory or regulatory restrictions on health insurers' ability to offer such incentives, or on offering differential premiums to those who are doing the right thing by themselves and other health fund members.

Much is made about the threat to community-rated private health insurance by offering supposedly preferential benefits and premium treatment to good behavers.[23] This misses the obvious point: the rated community is the pool of insured persons and their collective risk. If some of those persons work to reduce their risk of high-cost treatment and care, then over time the entire member pool benefits in terms of reduced benefit outlays and, if the scale of improvement is big enough, downward pressure on insurance premiums.

Commonwealth and state services

If a rewarded person is publicly-insured only, government could give them a lower Medicare safety net threshold, a lower Medicare levy, or larger tax concessions for medically-related expenses. Governments also could pay for non-Medicare covered prevention, condition management and related care, especially for those who are on the path

---

23 So much so that the Howard Government mistakenly allowed the Department of Health and Ageing to insert a highly-prescriptive definition of community rating in the *Private Health Insurance Act 2007*, with not a peep from the health insurance industry itself.

to improving their overall health.

Other tangible rewards include waiving or reducing a person's Medicare levy and lowering co-payments for Medicare and the PBS. More indirectly, governments could also increase the concessions on a person's overall taxable income to give them more cash in the hand – a 'good health tax dividend' for their documented efforts.

As direct operators of public hospitals, states and local hospital boards can also play their part by offering good behavers access to their services at concessional rates, and help individuals to manage their personal health risks. Indeed, that is what public sector coaching and condition management programs, such as Victoria's highly-successful Hospital Admissions Risk Programme, already do now. Indirectly, non-health state government services could be provided at reduced or no charge, recognising the good performer's lower net cost to scarce state resources. Such benefits could include discounted or free car registration as progress is reviewed annually.

Penalising poor behaviour

As Elphick's case highlights, imposing penalties reflecting individual choices is a political and ethical hot potato. No politician or clinician wants to be branded a killer because they prevent someone's access to care or services, or to be the first to question the universality of Medicare and 'free' access to public hospital services.

But encouraging more Australians to take more personal responsibility means sometimes turning the safety net into a high wire. If someone wilfully ignores scientific evidence and common sense, there should be no third-party obligation to indemnify them from the consequences. This should apply to both private and public health insurance.

Private health insurance

Health insurers need to be able to ensure that the vast majority of their members do not cross-subsidise outliers who choose to take big risks with their health. Community-rated private health insurance should not provide false comfort to the reckless, feckless, cupid and stupid – people like Harry Elphick and Donna Simpson.

With transparency and fairness, health insurers therefore should be able to:

- Set conditions of cover requiring members to undertake health assessments where risk factors are indicated and to take proactive (such as participating in a preventive or chronic disease management program) or remedial action (such as ceasing smoking in the light of a serious cardiac history) to reduce their risks of illness or injury
- Place a loading on premiums for members who do not participate in recommended support programs, or who do not meet reasonable compliance targets
- Consistent with life and disability insurance practice, decline to pay benefits, or pay reduced benefits, if an episode is related wholly or partly to the member's recklessness, fecklessness, cupidity or stupidity, and
- Have the discretion to refuse or terminate cover to a new applicant who pursues risky behaviours and refuses to modify them.

Commonwealth and state-subsidised health services

If private insurers can impose conditional cover and premium penalties on members, then Medicare, the Pharmaceutical Benefits Scheme and free public hospital treatment cannot become the last refuges of the reckless, feckless, cupid and stupid. Such behaviour should not be justified in terms of lip service to universal access: Commonwealth and state public payers, on their side of mutual obligation, therefore should be able to reserve the right to:

- Take a person's risk management behaviour into account when determining treatment priorities on public waiting lists
- Not pay the full or partial cost or scheduled benefit for an episode of treatment where clinical advice is that the individual has fully or partly brought the situation on her or himself
- Impose higher co-payments for Medicare and the PBS in

such episodes, and

- Allow public hospital boards and regional health services to charge public patients a significant co-payment for hospital and medical services fully or partly attributable to voluntary assumption of avoidable health risks.

Such consequences would need to be spelt out up-front and the community as a whole educated. Similarly, those patients (or their guardians) presenting at public hospital emergency departments with injuries arising from, not just alcohol and drug-fuelled causes, but also stupid behaviour in general, should also get the bill for their treatment, not the taxpayer. It would be the price of their selfish folly.

How could it work in practice?

Admittedly, such proposals would not be easy to administer. Decisions would be difficult and sensitive, and as the Elphick case indicates, would have ethical implications. Nevertheless, clinicians – general practitioners and other medical specialists – already are the gatekeepers to and de facto rationers of medical treatment.[24]   Their training and experience equips them to make difficult decisions about prioritising patients' access to, especially, hospital and surgical services.   This approach is simply an extension of that reality.

Gatekeeping would not change in a mutual obligation environment, but treating doctors receiving public income (including those receiving Medicare benefits and public hospital medical officers) also would have a duty of employment to assess whether a patient has assumed an avoidable risk voluntarily and the extent to which that choice has affected the patient's treatment requirements.[25] They would need to be statutorily indemnified against the legal consequences of exercising such judgments, and doubtful cases could be referred to a clinical board for a final opinion.

---

24 An issue that gives perennial ethical headaches for medical practitioners: for example A. Tauber, 'A Philosophical Approach to Rationing.' *The Medical Journal of Australia.* 179(9) 2003, 454-56.

25 Doctors in private practice claim that they are not employees: however, receiving income through the Medicare schedule creates a contractor-like relationship with the Commonwealth as payer.

If a patient's acute or chronic condition can reasonably be attributed to a patient's lifestyle or behavioural choices – such as excessive drinking or smoking, or morbid obesity with unhealthy diet and exercise patterns – that can be noted on a patient's medical record and advised to Medicare Australia, his private insurer or other payment authority. A patient's decisions to refuse or not comply with recommended health management advice can also be flagged. To mitigate the financial burdens of attributing financial responsibility to a patient or insured person, especially the less well-off, governments and private insurers could create a debt. This could then be paid off immediately or over time, with or without interest, in a manner similar to Higher Education Contribution Scheme obligations and using the same administrative machinery as HECS.

An alternative could be that the debt is recorded and collected by the funder as a priority creditor, in due course, from a person's estate. In this way the day of financial reckoning may perhaps be deferred for years in the future, but the overhanging debt would reflect the personal responsibility of the person incurring it.

Consistent with fairness principles advocated by Pearson and Lieber, however, any public or private penalty regime should allow for the funder waiving or discounting the incurred debt on compassionate or extreme hardship grounds. Indeed, for some individuals, it may be that the fright from the experience of being confronted by a penalty may 'scare them straight' in terms of their future health behaviours.

Conclusion

Most people know what is right and wrong when it comes to preventable injury and disease but far fewer follow through and apply such knowledge in their own lives.

As Mill stated famously in *On Liberty*, people should be free to do as they choose unless they have a detrimental effect on others.[26] If we blight our own lives voluntarily, that is our problem. But if others have to clean up behind us, including funding publicly subsidised and

---

26 J.S. Mill, *On Liberty*. In *John Stuart Mill: Three Essays*. Oxford: Oxford University Press, 1975, 68-69.

expensive treatment and care, our choices and behaviour affect others detrimentally too. In Mill's sense, that gives the state an interest which it can pursue or, at its discretion, set aside.

Promoting social justice in Australian healthcare means that we should offer a helping hand to our fellow citizens *but demand that they must also help themselves*. Someone taking responsibility for his own health deserves our help far more than those who do not, and public policy should encourage them to do so. Conversely, the reckless, feckless, cupid or stupid should not demand that taxpayers and fellow health insurance contributors must cover their costs unconditionally when they come to grief through their own choices and actions.

Put bluntly, turning access to publicly subsidised health care from unconditional entitlements to privileges governed by mutual obligation principles is more effective and fairer than the Marmot-inspired nostrums of the Australian Health Establishment. Let's give it a go!

11
Mutual obligation to welfare with responsibility

Asher Judah

The current focus on compliance attacks the dignity of income support recipients, denies their right to financial support, relieves the government of its obligations to recipients, and fails to produce benefits for recipients.

... the principle of eligibility according to need should be restored. Centrelink should not apply tests of merit (deservingness) to applicants for income support.[1]

Catholic Social Services, 2007

Welfare obligations in Australia are best understood as *mutual obligations*. Mutual obligation is based upon the principle that all Australians are entitled to welfare support when circumstances demand it. In exchange for this safety net, recipients are obligated to meet key responsibilities to themselves and the community which supports them. The concept of obligations linked to welfare is not new. It has existed in a variety of forms, mostly voluntary, for more than a century. The most contemporary interpretation, conditional welfare, made its first policy appearance in the 1980s in response to spiralling unemployment. Refined and expanded since then, conditional welfare obligations help to boost workplace participation and tackle welfare dependency.

Critics of conditional welfare argue that it is paternalistic and

---

1 Catholic Social Services, 'The Obligation is Mutual: Discussion Paper on Mutual Obligation.' October 2007, 26 and 29.

punitive. Their solution is to restore entitlements without responsibility and abolish the consequences of compliance breaches. History has proven that these approaches not only fail to alleviate poverty, but they end up causing more harm than good. This chapter examines the evolution of welfare obligations in Australia, whether they have worked, and who has opposed them and why. It also discusses the consequences of wind back, which presently threatens to undo recent successes, and concludes with reflections on future welfare obligation policy.

History of welfare obligations

Welfare obligations have developed through the introduction and evolution of tests applied by government to those receiving its support. Since the start of the 20th century, this process of trial and error has moved through five periods:

1. Pre-test period (laissez faire, the UK Minority Report on the Poor Laws and the 'wage earner' welfare state)
2. Work test period (rise of the welfare state)
3. Activity test period (advent of long-term unemployment and the birth of reciprocal obligation)
4. Workfare test period (mutual obligation and the centrality of employment to modern citizenship), and
5. Conduct test period (community intervention and income management).[2]

The pre-test period

Before the rise of the welfare state, 'the laissez faire solution to welfare dependency was to make claiming poor relief so difficult and unpleasant that the worst available job was better than life on relief.'[3] In the UK Minority Report for the Royal Commission on the Poor Laws and Relief of Distress 1905-09, mutual obligation was proposed as an alternative.[4]

---

2 Inspired by Catholic Social Services, 2007, 12.
3 Catholic Social Services, 2007, 4.
4 Beatrice Webb and Sidney Webb, *English Poor Law Policy*. London: Longmans, Green and Co. Second Impression 1913, 319.

Advocating a mixture of disciplinary training with the threat of punishment for failure to comply,[5] the Report claimed that 'social health is not a matter for the individual ... [or] Government alone, but depends essentially on the *joint responsibility* of the individual and the community for the maintenance of a definite minimum of civilised life.'[6] Put simply, it argued that the community had an obligation to prevent poverty, as well as to relieve it. Despite considerable debate, the Report's recommendations were never implemented.

At the same time, Australia adopted its own unique model for helping the poor.[7] This was undertaken by providing a living wage and modest welfare support through means-tested social security for the elderly, invalids and parents.[8] Castles aptly labelled this approach 'the wage earners' welfare state'.[9]

The work test period

During the Great Depression, government provided unemployment support called 'sustenance doles' to the masses of long-term unemployed.[10] It was during this period that the first tests appeared. Food and wages were often provided in exchange for public relief work.[11]

In the 1940s, the Welfare State was born. Means-tested child and family benefits, and support for the aged, widowed, sole parents, sick, disabled and unemployed were provided.[12] In the case of the unemployed, 'benefits were conditional on a person's availability to work and accept a suitable job'.[13]

---

5 Webb and Webb, 1913, 317.
6 Webb and Webb, 1913, 319. (emphasis added)
7 See discussion in Francis G. Castles, *The Working Class and Welfare, Reflections on the Political Development of the Welfare State in Australia and New Zealand 1890-1980*. Wellington, Allen & Unwin in association with Port Nicholson Press, 1985, 103.
8 Natalie Cooper, 'A Review of Australian Government Labour Market Policies Since 1945.' *HC Coombs Policy Forum*. Australian National University, 2011, 15.
9 Castles, 1985, 103.
10 Hilary Sawer, 'One Fundamental Value: Work for the Dole Participants' Views About Mutual Obligation.' PhD Thesis, RMIT University, March 2005, 11.
11 Sawer, 2005, 11.
12 Cooper, 2011, 15.
13 Cooper, 2011, 15.

The activity test period

Between 1950 and 1974, the unemployment rate never rose above three percent. However, between 1974 and 1983, it more than doubled and long-term unemployment resurfaced. Within ten years, 1983-1993, the unemployment rate rose to more than 10 percent with the long-term unemployed comprising one third. At the same time, the proportion of workforce age people receiving income support payments exploded, surging from five percent in 1974 to 17.6 percent in 1993.[14]

The growth of welfare dependency and the Government's inability to reduce long-term unemployment triggered several welfare reviews.[15] Their recommendations signaled the beginning of a shift in thinking from welfare being a 'responsibility light' entitlement to it becoming tied to increasingly specific obligations. The concept of reciprocal obligation was born and its arrival marked the beginning of the *activity test* period.[16] It also signified the resurrection of the conditional welfare ideas first advocated in the UK Minority Report.[17]

Key reforms during this period included:

- More active enforcement of unemployed job search efforts (including employment status registration)
- Replacement and strengthening of existing work, training and *activity tests*
- New reporting requirements to discourage young people from leaving education to pursue welfare, and
- Creation of 'activity agreements' which compelled participants to undertake training, work experience and return to work planning.

Despite these changes, welfare dependency and high unemployment lingered. In response, the Keating Labor Government intensified conditional welfare requirements through its *Working Nation* policy (1994). The primary reform came through the *Job Compact*. Under

---

14 Senator the Hon. Jocelyn Newman, 'The Challenge of Welfare Dependency in the 21st Century.' *Discussion Paper*. Department of Family and Community Services. 1999, 5.
15 Carney Report 1982 on youth unemployment, Kirby Report 1985 on employment services, and the Social Security Review 1985-88.
16 Partially inspired by the OECD's 'active society' agenda.
17 Catholic Social Services, 2007, 4.

the Compact, those receiving unemployment benefits for more than 18 months were offered individual case management, job readiness training, a job for 6-12 months, job search assistance[18] and a training wage which combined work and upskilling.[19] All these measures marked the next logical step in applying *activity tests*. If the government was prepared to provide increased support for recipients, then recipients needed to demonstrate a greater commitment to improve their circumstances.[20] The job offer element was critical. Refusal triggered a breach of reciprocal obligation requirements and risked the loss of benefits.[21]

The workfare test period

The 1996 election cut short the life of *Working Nation*. The newly-elected Coalition Government introduced its own version of conditional welfare. Entitled mutual obligation, its reforms discarded the failed elements of *Working Nation* and signalled the beginning of the *workfare test* era. The Coalition's mutual obligation policies are modelled upon the writings of conservative American political scientist, Lawrence Mead. Mead argued that the lack of behavioural enforcement within the welfare system was to blame for its growth and intractability: 'new benefits and services were given to the disadvantaged, but virtually no standards were set for how they should function in return.'[22] He claimed that welfare trapped people in a long-term dependency cycle where self reliance was eroded.[23]

Mead called for an end to passive welfare and introduction of welfare support accompanied by activities and financial penalties to ensure compliance.[24] His approach was to 'hassle and help' the disadvantaged out of their predicament. 'New paternalism' sought to

---

18 The Hon. Paul Keating MP, *Working Nation, The White Paper on Employment and Growth*. Canberra, Australian Government Publishing Service, May 1994a, Volume 1, 9.
19 Available only for some clients.
20 The Hon. Paul Keating MP, *Working Nation, Policies and Programs*. Australian Government Publishing Service, May 1994b, 116.
21 Keating 1994b, 9.
22 Lawrence M. Mead, *Beyond Entitlement, The Social Obligations of Citizenship*. New York: The Free Press, 1986, 49.
23 Lawrence M. Mead, 'Welfare Reform and the Family.' *Family Matters* No.54, Australian Institute of Family Studies, Spring/Summer 1999, 12.
24 Mead, 1986, 49.

build self-confidence, establish routines, prevent idleness, encourage self-discipline, develop work habits, change behaviour and establish dignity through work. The Coalition's *Work for the Dole* (WftD) scheme (1997) was Australia's first serious experiment with 'new paternalism'. Through imposition of *workfare tests*, *WftD* compelled young recipients to undertake specified activities as a condition of receiving support.[25] Using the philosophy of mutual obligation as a guide, the Coalition sought to create the elements Mead asserted were absent in the modern welfare system.

In 1999, the Howard Coalition Government commissioned the McClure inquiry into welfare reform. The McClure Report endorsed the Government's interventionist approach,[26] recommended extending *activity tests* to other recipients and encouraged sanctions for non-compliance.[27] It also called for a fundamental rethink of what responsibilities recipients had to the community which supported them.[28] Adopting many of the Report's recommendations, the Coalition sought to make the aspiration of employment for all able-bodied adults a central plank of good citizenship. *Australians Working Together* (2001), the *Active Participation Model* (2003) and *Welfare to Work* (2006) reforms each sought to recast society's attitude towards welfare and work. During the next six years, hundreds of thousands of Australians were subjected to *activity* and *workfare tests* as a condition of receiving welfare support. By learning from the shortcomings of former programs (including its own), the Coalition revolutionised welfare to work policy. Some of the more significant changes included:

- New participation requirements and activity choices were introduced for those receiving Newstart,[29] Parenting

---

25 Catholic Social Services, 2007, 3.
26 Patrick McClure, 'Participation Support for a More Equitable Society.' *Final Report of the Reference Group on Welfare Reform*. Canberra, July 2000, 5.
27 McClure, 2000, 40.
28 Cooper, 2011, 26.
29 Newstart Allowance is payable for eligible job seekers aged 21 years or over and under age pension age: Australian Bureau of Statistics, *2009-10 Year Book Australia, No. 91*, ABS Catalogue No. 1301.0, Canberra, 2010, 294.

Payments (PP),[30] Youth Allowance (YA),[31] and the Disability Support Pension (DSP).[32] Examples included:

- o Actively seeking employment accompanied by a job seeker diary
- o Accepting the first viable job offer ('work first')
- o Participation in the *WftD*, Green Corps and the Defence Force Reserves
- o Enrolment in *Job Search Training (JST)*, *Intensive Assistance* and career counselling
- o Performing voluntary work or part-time work
- o Undertaking further education or training to improve their labour market appeal
- o Attending fortnightly interviews with Centrelink, and
- o Agreeing to capacity assessments to determine DSP eligibility
- Expanding *WftD* to include unemployed people up to 50 years
- Stricter non-compliance penalties, and
- Greater scrutiny upon all welfare recipients.

The conduct test period

In mid-2007, mutual obligation underwent its next evolutionary change, *Conduct tests*. In response to the Northern Territory's report *Little Children are Sacred*,[33] a massive intervention into indigenous communities took place in the Northern Territory. The intervention

---

30 Parenting Payment is the main income support payment for people with sole or primary responsibility for the care of a young child. ABS, 2010, 294.

31 Youth Allowance supports young people aged 16–20 years actively seeking employment and full-time students aged 16–24 years. ABS, 2010, 299.

32 Disability Support Pension (DSP) is an income support payment for people with physical, intellectual or psychiatric impairment assessed as unable to work at least 15 hours a week independently of support: ABS, 2010, 296.

33 Rex Wild QC and Patricia Anderson, *Little Children are Sacred: Report of the Northern Territory Board of Inquiry into the Protection of Aboriginal Children from Sexual Abuse*. Northern Territory Government, 2007.

compelled parents in more than 20 indigenous communities[34] to meet specific obligations to their children in order to avoid PP's[35] being quarantined/managed on their behalf (Income Management).[36] According to the government, the aim was 'to extend the principle of mutual obligation beyond participation in the workforce to a range of behaviours that address, either directly or indirectly, the welfare and development of children.'[37] *Conduct tests* differed from previous mutual obligation policies in two ways. Whereas as *activity tests* and *workfare tests* had a strong labour market participation edge, *conduct tests* focussed upon family responsibilities. *Conduct tests* were also applied community-wide, rather than only to individuals.[38] Despite the Coalition losing government later that year, both the Rudd and Gillard Governments retained and later expanded *conduct tests*, albeit in a modified form.[39]

Have welfare obligations worked?

Determining whether welfare obligations have worked requires an assessment of three questions:

1. Has it boosted workforce participation?
2. Has it discouraged welfare dependency?
3. Have attitudes amongst welfare recipients changed?

Between 1997 and 2008, welfare obligations in Australia were substantially expanded. During this time, unemployment fell by more than 292 500 people,[40] long-term unemployed[41] dropped from 31.6 per

---

34 Peter Saunders, 'Australia from entitlement to employment.' *When Hassle Means Help, The International Lessons of Conditional Welfare*. London: Policy Exchange, 2008a, 19.
35 Parenting Payment and the Newstart.
36 Catholic Social Services, 2007, 12.
37 Mal Brough, House of Representatives Official Hansard, No. 11, August 7 2007, 10.
38 Catholic Social Services, 2007, 12.
39 Susanna Dunkerley, 'Labor Overhauls Welfare to Work in Federal Budget.' *The Australian*. May 10 2011; Lauren Wilson, 'Labor's New-Look Northern Territory Intervention.' *The Australian*. October 18 2011.
40 Australian Bureau of Statistics, *2000 Year Book Australia*, No. 82, ABS Catalogue No. 1301.0, 2000, Table 6.20, 123; ABS, 2010, Table 8.35, 256.
41 Lasting 52 weeks or more: ABS, 2010, 256.

cent[42] of total unemployment to 15 percent[43] and welfare recipients across Newstart, YA and PP declined by more than 900000.[44] Keeping in mind countervailing factors such population change, strong job creation and recipient movement onto activity-exempt welfare categories,[45] how much credit can these policies claim? Let us examine the facts.

According to a DEWR study in 2006, the *JST, Customised Assistance, Mutual Obligation* and *WftD* programs have each been effective in boosting employment.[46] All four programs helped the most disadvantaged find work,[47] many completely leaving welfare as a result of their participation.[48] In terms of net impacts, *JST* boosted employment outcomes by 11.2 percent, *Customised Assistance* by 10.1 percent, *Mutual Obligation* by 8.2 percent and *WftD* by 7.3 percent.[49] While not flawless, these outcomes were 'stronger than any achieved in previous programmes in Australia, and as good as any achieved overseas.'[50]

Program assessments of the 2006 *Welfare to Work* reforms, which tighten eligibility requirements and boosted *activity tests* for PP and DSP recipients (shifting many to Newstart), indicate that the changes have been positive. According to a 2008 DEEWR report, the PP reforms encouraged workforce participation and discouraged welfare dependency during their first twelve months of operations. For single principal carer parents on Newstart with a youngest child aged 8-15, 38 percent left welfare support after six months, primarily for employment.[51] This compares favourably with the previous three years where only 15 percent had done so.[52] For partnered principal carer parents on Newstart, 45 percent left after six months, compared with 32

42 ABS, 2010, 256.
43 ABS, 2000, 123.
44 ABS, 2000, Table 7.10, 161 and Table 7.13-7.14,164; ABS, *2002-Year Book Australia.* No. 84, ABS Catalogue No. 1301.0, 2002, Table 7.21, 173; ABS, 2010, Table 9.18, 295 and Table 9.21, 299.
45 E.g. Aged Pension.
46 Department of Employment and Workplace Relations, *Customised Assistance, Job Search Training, Work for the Dole and Mutual Obligation - A Net Impact Study.* Canberra, April 2006, 4.
47 DEWR, 2006, 4.
48 DEWR, 2006, 4.
49 DEWR, 2006, 3.
50 Saunders, 2008a, 14.
51 DEWR, *Welfare to Work Evaluation Report.* Canberra, May 2008, vi.
52 DEWR, 2008, vi.

percent in 2005-06.[53] Welfare dependency in this category also declined. People commencing on the PP (Single) and PP (Partnered) decreased by 30 percent and 32 percent respectively compared to the year before the reforms were introduced.[54]

Disappointingly, DSP reforms have been less effective in reducing overall dependency. This is largely due to *activity test* capacity assessments only being applied to 'new' recipients, not existing ones. For those affected, the results have been positive. Ten percent left income support after six months compared to only four percent in previous years.[55] Recipient growth also slowed.[56] More significant outcomes could be possible if all DSP recipients were subjected to the same capacity assessments.

Triggering a permanent shift in recipient behaviour is another critical test of effectiveness. Despite constant complaint from welfare organisations about the negative implications of mutual obligation, the vast majority of job seekers have embraced it. In a Centrelink survey in 2001, 85 percent agreed with the idea of mutual obligation.[57] In 2002, 60 percent felt their involvement in *WftD* had improved their chances of getting a job.[58] Even penalties have been embraced. According to the Social Policy Research Centre, 80 percent of non-compliant recipients agreed that 'it's fair to breach people who aren't doing the right thing.'[59] 'Nearly 90 percent of breached customers reported increased participation in a range of compliance'[60] after being penalised. '[M]ore than two-fifths said they found some kind of work or increased existing hours of work'[61] as a result of penalties.

By placing increased responsibilities upon welfare recipients, mutual obligation has improved employment outcomes, discouraged

53 DEWR, 2008, vi.

54 DEWR, 2008, v-vi.

55 DEWR, 2008, vii.

56 Peter Yeend, *Budget 2011–12: Disability Support Pension – Reforms.* Canberra: Parliamentary Library, 19 May 2011.

57 Department of Workplace Relations, *Participation and Obligations: Findings from the 2002 Job Seeker Survey.* Canberra, 2002, 3.

58 DWR, 2002, 6.

59 Tony Eardley, The Impact of Breaching on Income Support Recipients.' *Social Policy Research Centre.* Newsletter 91 November 2005, Figure 1, 7.

60 Eardley, 2005, 6.

61 Eardley, 2005, 6.

dependency and changed recipient attitudes towards welfare and work. While not without its shortcomings, mutual obligation has achieved some valuable breakthroughs in the notoriously difficult area of welfare policy.

Critics of welfare obligation

Opponents of welfare obligation policies have never truly accepted that welfare recipients have responsibilities to the community which supports them. Their opposition is borne out of two disagreements which rest at the heart of mutual obligation's effectiveness – paternalism and penalty-driven compliance.

Critics of paternalism argue that welfare obligations represent a conservative assault upon the individual liberty of society's most disadvantaged members. Their views stem from the belief that 'government-protected minimum standards of income, nutrition, health, housing and education'[62] are provided to every citizen as a political right rather than as an act of charity.[63] Consequently, when entitlement is replaced with conditionality, as it is under mutual obligation, they view it as a direct threat to the personal freedoms and interests of welfare recipients. According to its advocates, the imposition of *activity tests*, *workfare tests*, *conduct tests* and 'work first' requirements erode personal freedoms and place the rights-based welfare system at risk.[64] Whereas in the past the recipient had the power to choose how best to improve his/her welfare status, under mutual obligation that power has been usurped by the state.

According to Catholic Social Services, mutual obligation is 'an exercise in selective paternalism.'[65] It is selective in that it singles out individuals or groups based on social disadvantage[66] and it is paternalistic because it 'rests on the assumption that policy makers

---

62 H. Wilensky, *The Welfare State and Equality*. University of California Press, Berkeley, 1975 as cited in The Society of St Vincent de Paul, (Abstract) 'Time to Re-frame: Understanding the War Against Welfare, Road to Where?' *The Politics and Practice of Implementing Welfare-to-Work' Forum*. 2006, 4.
63 Wilensky, 2006, 4.
64 Socialist Alliance, *Welfare Rights Charter*. Ultimo, August 2007, 1-2.
65 Catholic Social Services, 2007, 10.
66 Catholic Social Services, 2007, 10.

are more rational and more moral than income support recipients.'[67]
This analysis is essentially correct. Mutual obligation policy represents
enforcement of behavioural standards upon individuals and/or groups
whom government believes are trapped in a 'culture of fatalism'.[68] By
forcing the disadvantaged to undertake specified activities, mutual
obligation seeks to do for them that which they are deemed to be
incapable of doing themselves. As Mead notes:

People who live without limits soon sacrifice their own interests
to immediate gratifications. To live effectively, people need personal
restraint to achieve their own long-run goals. In this sense, obligation
is the precondition of freedom. Those who would be free must first be
bound. And if people have not been effectively bound by functioning
families and neighbourhoods in their formative years, government must
attempt to provide the limits later, imperfect though they must be.[69]

Unfortunately, it is this 'new paternalism' of which critics most
passionately disapprove. Catholic Welfare Australia claims it is
'inherently unfair',[70] the Brotherhood of St Laurence reports that
the tests are counterproductive to securing employment[71] and others
argue that the preference for work above all else erodes parenting
choices.[72] Despite coming from differing philosophical perspectives,
critics believe that if recipients were left to their own devices, they
would prove themselves capable of acting in their own best interests.
Sadly, this approach has a devastating legacy. Rights-focused welfare
policy flourished in the absence of a viable alternative between 1975
and 1994. The end result was record high unemployment, long-term
unemployment and intergenerational welfare dependency. Despite

---

67 Catholic Social Services, 2007, 20.
68 Peter Saunders, 'A Whiff of Compassion? The Attack on Mutual obligation.' *Issue Analysis*. No. 96, Centre for Independent Studies, 10 June 2008b, 7.
69 Lawrence M. Mead, *The New Paternalism, Supervisory Approaches to Poverty*. Washington: Bookings Institution Press, 1997, 23.
70 Catholic Welfare Australia (Catholic Social Services), *Catholic Welfare Australia's position on the AWT Bill: Febuary 2003*. Curtin, 2003, 2.
71 Brotherhood of St Laurence, The Society of St Vincent de Paul and University of Melbourne Centre for Public Policy, *Much Obliged Disadvantaged Job Seekers' Experiences of the Mutual Obligation Regime*. Fitzroy, 2003, 38.
72 Eva Cox, 'Welfare: Government Fails its Social Democracy Obligations.' http://www.crikey.com.au/2011/05/11/welfare-government-fails-its-social-democracy-obligations/, May 2011.

the best of intentions, liberty and compassion have never proven an adequate match for the seductiveness of welfare without responsibility. Compulsion, despite its drawbacks, must also play a part.

The second thread of opposition to welfare obligations relates to its punitive characteristics. Critics argue that that the principle of eligibility according to 'need' has been replaced with that of 'merit' (or deservedness through tests and obligations).[73] Its advocates claim that a shift in the moral and political assumptions underpinning the welfare system has occurred to the detriment of its recipients.[74] Consequently, the disadvantaged now face harsher treatment simply to maintain their basic welfare rights. Supporters of this view argue that obligation tests focus too much upon punishment at the expense of assistance. Rather than being provided a hand up, they are being slapped down.[75] ACOSS, for instance, argues that *conduct tests* inflict 'shame and indignity on income support recipients,[76] the Society of St Vincent de Paul asserts mutual obligation demeans the needy[77] and the National Welfare Rights Network claims that *activity tests* lead to fatigue and disillusionment.[78]

Concerns about welfare obligations do not end there. Critics remain vehemently opposed to using coercion to encourage compliance. Punitive measures, such as reductions or suspensions of payments, are opposed on the grounds that they are 'excessively harsh'[79] and force recipients to turn to crime.[80] Critics also argue that they invariably

---

73 Catholic Social Services, 2007, 26.

74 Jeremy Moss, 'Ethics, Politics & Mutual Obligation.' *The Australian Journal of Social Issues*. Volume 36(1), February 2001.

75 Correspondence from Jobs Australia CEO Mr David Thompson to the Minister for Employment Participation, Jobs Australia, Carlton South, February 13 2008, 2.

76 Australian Council of Social Service, *ACOSS Opening Statement*. Senate Community Affairs Legislation Committee Inquiry into the Social Security and Other Legislation Amendment (Welfare Reform and Reinstatement of the Racial Discrimination Act) Bill 2009 and Related Bills. Canberra, 26 February 2010, 1.

77 The Society of St Vincent de Paul, *Social justice is Undermined by Demonisation of the Disadvantaged*. Canberra, March 2002, 3.

78 National Welfare Rights Network, *Kicking Them While They're Down ...Youth Allowance and Youth Poverty*. Sydney, June 2002, 38.

79 Dennis Pearce, Julian Disney and Heather Ridout, *The Independent Review of Breaches and Penalties in the Social Security System*. Canberra, March 2002, Section 7.8.

80 Brotherhood of St Laurence, *The Community Expects ... Public Opinion About Breach Penalties for Unemployed People*. Fitzroy, June 2002, 1.

harm the innocent (families),[81] and have little tolerance for the unique circumstances of the disadvantaged.

While there may be an element of truth to these claims, such situations remain clearly in the minority.

In order to correct the injustice of punitive action, critics call for it to be softened or abolished. Their motivation is simple. 'Significant behaviour change depends on an element of compulsion, backed by financial sanctions.'[82] If these components can be removed or weakened, then mutual obligation will not work. Compliance penalty critics know this. That is why they relentlessly pursue its demise. For them, the 'rights agenda' remains paramount. It has always been better for the disadvantaged to remain listless but free, than to be held to account for their bad habits. This is one of the most significant failings of left-wing social policy.[83] It forsakes responsibility and consequence for liberal purity.

The threat of wind back

Despite evidence in support of mutual obligation, many critics remain. By rejecting meaningful state intervention, they champion a return to the model of unconditional welfare which existed decades ago. For much of the Coalition's tenure, this approach fell upon deaf ears. In 2007, however, a government with a sympathetic attitude was elected. From their first budget, a subtle but purposeful wind back of welfare obligations commenced, including:

- Doubling the time period a person may remain unemployed before they must commence *WftD* activities
- Weakening the obligations upon PP recipients to find employment
- Shifting the focus towards skills training at the expense of 'work first', and
- Softening the penalty regime for activity failures, including:

---

81 Catholic Welfare Australia, 2003, 2.
82 Peter Saunders, 2008a, 21.
83 Mark Latham MP, 'The Myths of the Welfare State'. Keynote presentation. Brisbane: Institute of Public Administration Australia, Queensland Division, July 14 2001, 7.

- o Replacing income suspension with 'no show, no pay' penalties
- o Greater discretion for the Job Network to report 'participation failures
- o Softening the enforcement provisions behind the eight-week non-payment period rule, and
- o Creating hardship provisions to alleviate the impact of serious failure penalties.

During the past two decades, Australia has incrementally refined its welfare system to become one of the most effective in the world at moving the disadvantaged from welfare to work.[84] By weakening the principles underpinning *workfare*, 'work first', *activity tests* and penalty driven compliance, the Labor Government is sabotaging the elements which make that system work. Mutual obligation policies are effective specifically because they strike the correct balance between support and structure. The Government should be careful not to undo that which has developed over decades of painful trial and error.

Future areas of welfare obligation reform

In lieu of restoring the obligations and penalties which were in effect prior to 2007, there are two areas where welfare obligations could be expanded.

Removal of DSP grandfathering

As part of the 2006 *Welfare to Work* reforms, the Coalition tightened the eligibility requirements for recipients of DSPs to address its exponential (and suspect) growth (up 113 percent since 1991).[85] The reform compelled anyone deemed capable of working at least 15 hours per week to switch to Newstart or YA and undertake modified activity requirements including looking for work. It also aimed to close the

---

84 Saunders, 2008a, 14.
85 Department of Families, Housing, Community Services and Indigenous Affairs, *Statistical Paper No. 9: Income Support Customers: a Statistical Overview 2010*. Canberra, 2010, Table 6, 9.

loophole on recipients switching categories to gain financial advantage[86] and/or avoid mutual obligation requirements.[87] Similar to other *workfare test* initiatives, this reform sought to bring DSP obligations into line with other welfare categories. Unfortunately, it was not introduced retrospectively. Existing DSP recipients were 'exempt' whereas 'new' recipients were not. This had two consequences:

1. *Workfare tests* were applied inequitably to the same recipient group, and
2. Welfare dependency amongst moderately impaired DSP recipients remained unaddressed.

In June 2006, the total number of DSP recipients was 712,163.[88] Since then, it has increased by 80,418 people,[89] growing at an average rate of 3-4 percent each year.[90] Setting aside those who have died, found work, moved onto aged pensions or have ceased to receive welfare, a sizeable number of people remain exempt from the new obligations as a result of the grandfathering provision.

In May 2011, the Gillard Government sought to address this by announcing new obligations for all DSP recipients aged less than 35 deemed capable of working eight hours a week. From July 1 2012, all will be compelled to attend quarterly interviews and develop 'participation plans' to encourage workforce entry.[91] While this reform is well-intentioned, it is unlikely to work. Under the reform, 'participation plan' compliance remains voluntary. As a result, most recipients are unlikely to follow through with them. History has repeatedly shown that programs such as this only work if they are supported by compulsion and punitive measures. In this case, the Government has not applied this lesson.

Many policy experts have advocated an extension of mutual obligation

---

86 Yeend, 2011.
87 Saunders, 2008a, 14-15.
88 FaHCSIA, 2010.
89 FaHCSIA, 2010.
90 Department of Family and Community Services, *Improving Employment Opportunities for People with a Disability*. Canberra, March 2003, 5.
91 The Hon. Jenny Macklin MP, Minister for Families, Housing, Community Services and Indigenous Affairs, 'Supporting Australians with Disability into Work.' *Media Release*. May 10 2011.

to more DSP recipients to address the category's shortcomings.[92] The Harmer Report into pension reform calls for 'improved assessment procedures to ensure that people are not inappropriately placed on [DSP].'[93] These recommendations should be followed up.

English language obligations for new Australians

Each year, thousands of people migrate to Australia from nations where English is not the dominant language. This openness finds its roots in Australia's history of supporting immigration to meet its economic, social, demographic and ethical responsibilities. Despite its many challenges, migration from non-English speaking background populations remains essential to our long-term success.

Unfortunately, many migrants arrive without functional English,[94] especially through our humanitarian programs. According to the *Report of the Review of Settlement Services for Migrants and Humanitarian Entrants*, 'learning English is one of the most important steps that non-English speaking people can take towards full participation in Australian society.'[95] English language skills are increasingly critical to securing employment, accessing government services, avoiding social isolation, and for understanding one's legal rights. Indeed, language barriers are amongst the greatest obstacles to successful settlement. An immigrant who cannot speak English is more than five times more likely to be unemployed after six months in Australia than one who does. Twelve months later, this ratio worsens.[96]

Extending mutual obligation principles to elements of Australia's migration program is one solution to this integration challenge. Indeed,

---

92 Jessica Brown, 'Working Towards Self-Reliance: Three Lessons for Disability Pension Reform.' *CIS Policy Monograph*. No. 124, 2011, 10; Saunders, 2008a, 15.

93 Jeff Harmer, *Pension Review Report*. Canberra: Department of Families, Housing, Community Services and Indigenous Affairs, February 2009, 143.

94 Functional English is defined as being able to use English well enough to deal with everyday social situations and some work situations. Source: Department of Immigration and Multicultural and Indigenous Affairs, *Report of the Review of Settlement Services for Migrants and Humanitarian Entrants*. Canberra: Department of Immigration and Multicultural and Indigenous Affairs, May 2003, 255.

95 DIMIA, 2003, 253.

96 Department of Immigration and Citizenship, *Fact Sheet 14 - Migrant Labour Market Outcomes*. Canberra, 2010, Table 3.

it is an approach currently being examined in the United Kingdom, and is already in place in France and Germany. Australian policy-makers should explore the imposition of obligations upon immigrants to undertake the Adult Migrant English Program (AMEP) as a mandatory prerequisite for future welfare support. AMEP has historically been an 'optional' component of mutual obligation. This should be revisited in cases of extreme language disadvantage. Such an outcome would enhance their capacity to integrate with the broader community. It would also boost their prospects for successful settlement. A review of this policy area should be encouraged.

Conclusion

Welfare obligations have undergone a remarkable transformation in Australia during the past century. Transitioning from an era without any tests to one entirely defined by them, obligations now rest at the heart of our welfare system. Through the process of trial and error, the evolution of welfare obligations has shown that liberty and compassion alone are not enough to overpower the seductiveness of welfare without responsibility. Only imposition of obligations, backed up by threat of sanctions, has been successful in achieving lasting change.

In the mid-2000s, the Government got this balance right. In recent years, a new government has been experimenting with the notion of wind back. Such a flirtation should be avoided. Instead, the Government should begin examining ways to extend the successful principles of mutual obligation to other elements of Australia's expansive welfare system. Helping the moderately disabled secure employment and new Australians learn functional English are two areas worth considering. Despite its many critics, mutual obligation has always been about improving outcomes for the disadvantaged. By providing dignity through discipline and structure, mutual obligation seeks to empower the poor by creating obligations which enable their freedom.

12
Helping real refugees

Mirko Bagaric

'It is unintended cruelty to give finite refugee places to strategic travelers in preference to the most destitute people on earth'.
- Mirko Bagaric

Refugee settlement is based on compassion

Australia caps its refugee intake to no more than 13,750 people per year. This is almost a negligible number for an opulent nation of 21 million people to absorb. Despite this, the manner in which Australia processes refugees has become a headline and divisive political and social issue. Lost in the debate is an important paradox that concerns refugee policy.

Nearly all immigration to western countries, including Australia, is based on what immigrants can do for the country. Hence countries readily admit highly skilled people who can add value to the economic infrastructure of the country and cashed-up tourists who inject money directly into the local economy. Refugee settlement stands apart from this: it is based on compassion. It focuses on what we can do for desperate and needy strangers. It is the principal manifestation of our compassion towards non-Australians. The arrival of each refugee arrival should be celebrated. It is not. The issue has become politicized. The focus is on stopping 'refugee smugglers', as opposed to the lives that are enhanced by becoming part of the Australian community. A humane policy has turned into a focal point of political and social acrimony.

There are a number of benchmarks against which refugee policy should be assessed. The refugee intake should be systematic, transparent, orderly and dictated by the level of need of applicants. Current Australian government policy on refugees fares poorly on these criteria. It is probably the most complex, artificial, expensive and strained in the world. Certainly it is the only country that has excised part of its soil for refugee purposes[1] and which is seeking to delegate its refugee obligations to other nations such as Malaysia.[2] The cost is greatly increased by the process of mandatorily detained illegal arrivals.

In this chapter, I suggest a solution to the refugee problem. In essence, it involves picking refugees on the basis of their level of need. Where the need is approximately equal, those who have been waiting longest for refugee resettlement should get priority. Australia should take its entire refugee intake from people warehoused in refugee camps. It should cease processing refugees who arrive at our shores (whether by sea or air) without pre-determined refugee recognition.

This would mean an end to mandatory detention and the process would be orderly and humane – the main criterion for acceptance would move to 'need', as opposed to those that are the most 'pushy' and mobile. This would require Australia to redefine the meaning of a refugee and possibly withdraw from the Refugees Convention. At the same time, Australia should increase its refugee intake to at least double the current quota.

Much of the commentary on the refugee issue has been misinformed and reflexive. A key failing has been a misunderstanding of the meaning of a refugee and the ethical problems inherent in this definition. This has led to most commentators assuming that this definition should continue to be adopted, thereby proposing a solution with an unstable foundation. The problems, predictably, compound from there. The next part of the chapter provides an overview of what it means to be a refugee. I then set out the reality of the refugee crisis in numbers, locally and internationally. After proposing a preferable definition, suggest an

---

1 Especially Christmas Island, which the most popular destination for boat arrivals.
2 Although the High Court in *Plaintiff M70/2011 v Minister for Immigration and Citizenship; Plaintiff M106 of 2011 v Minister for Immigration and Citizenship [2011] HCA 32* stated that it was unlawful to send refugees to Malaysia, at the date of writing this paper the federal government was proposing changes to the *Migration Act 1958* (Cth) which would facilitate this transfer.

orderly way forward.

History and background to the refugees convention

The criteria that Australia applies to determine refugee eligibility is taken from the 1951 Convention Relating to the Status of Refugees (the Convention), which has been picked by the *Migration Act* 1958 (Cth). These criteria and the protection obligations under the Convention form the core elements of refugee law and practice.

The Convention was drafted following the uprooting of masses of people as a result of World War II. The Convention was adopted by a special United Nation Conference on July 28 1951, and entered into force on April 21 1954.[3] It was drafted between 1948 and 1951 by a combination of United Nations organs, ad hoc committees and a conference of plenipotentiaries, at which twenty-six states were represented.[4] Unlike earlier refugee instruments, the 1951 Convention purported to provide a *general* definition of who was to be considered a refugee.

Despite its universal overtones, the 1951 Convention was limited by the fact that it protected mainly Europeans fleeing after World War II.[5] Furthermore, the definition of a refugee set out in Article 1A(2) of the Convention defined refugees only in terms of those who had a well-founded fear of being persecuted 'as a result of events occurring before January 1 1951'. These restrictions were removed and the definition was expanded by the 1967 Protocol relating to the Status of Refugees.[6] Accession to the 1967 Protocol enabled states to apply the substantive provisions of the Convention to refugees as defined by the Convention, but without the temporal and geographic limitations. Hence, the Convention now applies to all persons who are refugees

---

3 G Goodwin-Gill, *The Refugee in International Law*. Oxford University Press (2nd edition) 1996, 4.

4 J Hathaway, *The Law of Refugee Status* (1991), 6. For a history of the process leading to the drafting of the convention, see P Weis, *The Refugee Convention, 1951: The Travaux Preparatoires Analysed*. 1995. Note the earlier international agreements entered into on behalf of refugees are referred to in article 1A(1) of the Convention.

5 Goodwin-Gill, 1996, 19. Note that the definition included an optional geographical limitation that permitted States, on ratification, to limit their obligations to refugees from 'events occurring within Europe' prior to the critical date – Article 1B.

6 Hathaway, 1991, 10.

because of events occurring at *any time*. Denmark was the first state to ratify the 1951 Convention (in 1952). Since then, more than 140 states have acceded to the Convention.[7]

The normative overtone of the Convention glosses over the fact that it was developed and entered into mainly to assist European refugees, and to serve Western political and economic needs.[8] This is a point emphasised by James Hathaway:

> The two main characteristics of the Convention refugee definition are its strategic conceptualisation and its Eurocentric focus. The strategic dimension of the definition comes from successful efforts of western states to give priority in protection matters to persons whose flight was motivated by pro-Western political values. As anxious as the Soviets had been to exclude political emigres from the scope of the Convention for fear of exposing their weak flank, so the more numerous and more powerful western states were preoccupied to maximise the international visibility of that migration. ... The refugee definition was carefully phrased to include only persons who have been disenfranchised by their state on the basis of race, religion, nationality, membership of a particular social group, or political opinion, matters in regard to which eastern bloc practice has historically been problematic. Western vulnerability in the area of respect for human rights, in contrast, centers more on the guarantee of socio-economic human rights, than on respect for civil and political rights. Unlike the victims of civil and political oppression, however, persons denied even such basic rights as food health care or education are excluded from the international refugee regime (unless that deprivation stems from civil or political status). By mandating protection for those whose (Western inspired) socio-economic rights are at risk, the Convention adopted an incomplete and politically partisan human rights rationale.[9]

Thus the history of the Convention reflects the fact that the plight of displaced or 'needy' people was subordinated to the strategic objectives

---

7 Department of Immigration and Multicultural and Indigenous Affairs, *Interpreting the Refugees Convention – An Australian Contribution*. 2002, 1.
8 Hathaway, 1991, 6.
9 Hathaway, 1991, 7-8.

of the state parties who drafted the Convention. The criteria for refugee status was defined by reference to the interests of nation states pre-occupied with Cold War politics.[10]

Article 1A(2) of the Convention states a refugee is any person who:

> … owing to well-founded fear of being persecuted for reasons of race, religion, nationality, membership of a particular social group or political opinion, is outside the country of his nationality and is unable, or owing to such fear, is unwilling to avail himself of the protection of that country, or who, not having a nationality and being outside the country of his former habitual residence as a result of such events, is unable or, owing to such fear, is unwilling to return to it.

The core aspect of the definition of a refugee is that it is limited to protecting people who face harm for one (or more) of five narrow and specific 'grounds', being either their race, nationality, religion, political opinion or membership of a distinct social group. Moreover, it only protects people who leave their country of origin and manage to enter another county. It therefore excludes people who are facing imminent death in their country as a result of famine, natural disaster or military action.

If a person meets the refugee definition, a range of rights and protections pursuant to the Convention is conferred on her or him. The most important of which is non-refoulement (non-return) to the state from which she or he has fled.[11]

Refugee numbers are capped in Australia and refugee number realities

The Australian Government has capped the number of humanitarian visa places at 13,750. Refugees take the vast majority of these places. The ceiling has remained relatively steady over the past few years – fluctuating by only a few hundred.

The Australian refugee intake has two main components. Those who

---

10 Hathaway, 1991, 232-233.
11 Article 3 confers a right to not be discriminated against; Article 4 covers freedom of religion; Article 16 provides for free access to the courts; Article 21 provides a right to housing; Article 22 provides a right to access to education. See also, articles 21, 23, 26 and 32.

come to Australia without pre-existing refugee determination (by land or sea) and those taken offshore, from locations such as refugee camps. People taken offshore must satisfy the refugee definition or qualify under the slightly broader Special Humanitarian Program which relates to people outside their home country who are subject to a gross violation of human rights in their home country.[12]

Each visa taken by an applicant who arrives in Australia by boat or plane is one less place available for offshore applicants, in places like refugee camps – and vice versa. If the entire quota is filled by onshore applicants, no offshore applicants can be admitted. Thus, while there is no refugee queue, there are a finite number of spots. In 2009-10, 9,236 visas were granted pursuant to the offshore component and 4,534 visas were granted for onshore applicants.[13]

The number of onshore applicants is rapidly increasing, since the Labor Government, after sweeping into power in 2007, abolished temporary visas for refugees and processing in Naru. For the 2010-11 year only 6,000 of the 13,770 places had been allocated for offshore applicants, while 7,750 were for onshore.[14]

In the 2009-10 year, 8,749 people were placed into immigration detention, double the number of the previous years. Of these people 81 percent were unauthorised arrivals – with about three-quarters of these arriving by boat and the balance by aeroplane. The others were people who overstayed or otherwise breached their visa conditions. At June 30 2010 there were 4,077 people in immigration detention. This is a fourfold increase from the previous year and is mainly attributable to the large increase in boat arrivals during the year.

In 2010 more than 6,879 asylum seekers arrived by boat, thrusting themselves into our sphere of moral concern.[15] In the process they wantonly faded out from our radar the needs of often more desperate

---

12 This definition is substantially narrower than that proposed below because applicants must still be outside their country of origin and does not apply to those in life-threatening situations as a result of natural events, such as famine and natural disasters.

13 Department of Immigration and Citizenship, *Fact Sheet 60 – Australia's Refugee and Humanitarian Program.* (undated).

14 DIAC, (undated).

15 Janet Phillips and Harriet Spinks, *Boat Arrivals in Australia Since 1976.* Australian Parliamentary Library. 2011, appendix A.

asylum seekers, most of whom are 'warehoused' in camps. This number of boat arrivals grew rapidly under the Kevin Rudd/Julia Gillard regime, that is, since 2008. The number of people that came by boat during the past few years has leapt from one in 2002 to nearly 7,000 in 2010.[16]

Tellingly, approximately 80 percent of the people arriving by boat to Australia are from Afghanistan, Iran, Iraq or Sri Lanka. These people are from half way around the world. None of them stumbles into Australia. They make a deliberate, educated and reasoned decision to come to Australia as opposed to dozens of other countries that are more accessible to them.

The increased rate of asylum seeker arrivals is not reflected internationally, where refugee numbers have remained relatively stable – at about 14 million for a decade.[17]

It is interesting to note that on the basis of contribution per capita, Australia is the fifteenth most substantial donor country to international refugee aid agencies. In absolute terms, it is the thirteenth most generous donor country. In per capita terms, the 10 most generous countries are Luxembourg, Norway, Sweden, Denmark, Liechtenstein, Ireland, the Netherlands, Finland, Switzerland and Monaco. The United States is 14th on the list.[18]

Australia is in fact the most generous country on earth in terms of resettling refugees who do not come to its shores. There is no obligation on countries to bring refugees to it shores. Australia is one of the few nations that proactively engage in this process. The top five nations and the ratio of settled refuges to host country population are Australia (1: 2,400); Canada (1: 3,100); Sweden (1: 4,200); United States (1: 5,100); and Norway (1: 5,300).[19]

If the boat numbers continue to increase at current levels, soon all of the 13,750 places will be taken by those whose only basis for accelerated refugee determination is the temerity to command our attention and the resources to come to our shores at their choosing. While the government can nominally allocate only a certain portion of the 13,750 places to

---

16 Phillips and Spinks, 2011, appendix A.
17 US Committee for Refugees, *World Refugee Survey 2009*, 2009, 4.
18 USCR, 2009, 28.
19 USCR, 2009, 29.

onshore applicants, the reality is that if more refugees come than the onshore quota, the government cannot reject then and hence they will eat into the offshore quota.

This equates to continued brutality for the more than eight million asylum seekers that have been warehoused in refugee camps for over 10 years. More than 90 percent of them are in countries with per capita incomes of less than $10,000, such as Syria, Pakistan and Venezuela.

In the next section, it is contended that it is an abuse of the rights accorded by the Convention for a country to grant its limited refugee places to strategic travelers over those whose lives are in imminent peril and who do not have resources to make travel.

The Convention protects only people suffering because of arbitrary reasons and those who leave their country

The key proposition to my reform proposal is that the five Convention grounds should be abolished. They are arbitrary and hence discriminatory: there is no relevant basis for giving preferential treatment to a person who is 'persecuted' because of his or her political or religious beliefs, nationality or group membership as distinct from a person who suffers serious harm for economic or other reasons.

The only way to treat people equally in this respect is not to focus on the *reason* for the persecution, but *the extent of the need* for asylum. The only universal criteria for sympathy and compassion are *need* and *pain*. Thus, it follows that state assistance and protection should be accorded to those most bereft of the resources and opportunities that are a pre-condition to human survival and flourishing. This raises difficult questions about the hierarchy of human needs and wants. However, human biology mandates that the most important needs are food, shelter, security of person and liberty. People who are denied these should be considered as refugees – irrespective of the reason for the deprivation.

The main defect with the Convention is that the existing five grounds do not come close to identifying the minimum conditions necessary for human subsistence. The right to express which political party or political ideology one prefers, for example, is of little use unless one has food and shelter. Further, it is regrettable (if not offensive) that all that is important in a person's life can turn on the interpretation of a throw-away line, such as 'particular social group'.

This leads to a more pervasive and fundamental problem with the Convention. Not only is it not based on a needs criterion, it is not based on *any* overarching principle at all. There is no underlying rationale which unifies the grounds and which justifies why they are of greater importance than other human concerns. As a result – blind allegiance to the Convention aside – a causal connection between persecution and a convention ground does not provide a normative reason for compliance with the Convention. Absent an explanation for why the Convention grounds are more important than other human interests, the Convention definition of 'refugee' is arbitrary and ultimately discriminatory – it gives a preference to those falling within the grounds on the basis of an irrelevant difference.

In light of universal principles governing the commitment to all humankind, why should any state be concerned about complying with the Convention? The answer is that from the normative perspective (that is, international law obligations aside), relatively speaking it should care very little – sending money to the starving in Africa would be a far better use of resources. It is not surprising, then, that Goodwin-Gill has noted that given the narrow framework of the Convention, which was not intended to provide for universal refugee solutions, it 'is remarkable … that the 1951 Convention still attracts both ratifications and support among States from all regions.'[20]

An alternative definition

The only way the Convention can be reformed to circumvent such criticisms is to select universal features of humankind as the cornerstone for refugee status.

The new definition should appeal to irreducible sociological and normative considerations. Assistance should be limited to people whose lives are in peril as a result of lack of food, water or shelter, or who have a real fear of having their physical integrity or liberty violated. This, effectively, means that the principal right recognised in the proposed definition is the right to life. The only concession that should be made

---

20 Goodwin-Gill, 1996, 297.

to confining assistance to threats to life is to recognise the importance of personal liberty, which while not as fundamental to the right to life, is essential for human beings to attain any semblance of fulfilment. The importance of liberty to the human species is reflected by the fact that deprivation of it constitutes the gravest form of punishment that is inflicted by Western cultures against wrongdoers (apart from many parts of the United States where capital punishment is still sanctioned).

In light of the above discussion, the definition of refugee that should be adopted is as follows. A refugee is a person who owing to:

- the fact that his or her life is in peril as a result of lack of food, water or shelter, or
- a well-founded fear of having his or her physical integrity or liberty violated,
- is outside the country of his or her nationality and is unable to avail himself or herself of the relevant resources or protection of that country; or who, not having a nationality and being outside the country of his or her former habitual residence, is unable or unwilling to return to it.[21]

Thousands of people continue to die daily of hunger and other readily preventable causes. At the time of writing this chapter, parts of Somalia, Kenya and Ethiopia were experiencing a major famine with more than 13 million people in need of urgent aid. Most of these people are too impoverished to manage to hobble over a border or two. It is manifestly cruel to discriminate against them as far as migration places are concerned on the basis that they suffer in their homeland, instead of in another country. Thus, the necessity for people to leave their homeland to qualify for a refugee visa should also be abolished.

Rather than paying homage to the Convention as the basis for our humanitarian intake, Australia should take a leading role in broadening the scope of people it will allow to migrate for reasons of need. For the purposes of our domestic law, we need to broaden the definition of a

---

21 This has some similarities with the UN definition for internally displaced people: persons who have been forced to flee their homes suddenly or unexpectedly in large numbers, as a result of armed conflict, internal strife, systematic violations of human rights or natural or man-made disasters, [and who are within the territory of their own country]': *Analytical Report of the Secretary-General on Internally Displaced Persons*, E/CN 4/19992/93, February 14 1992, paragraph 17.

refugee so that our compassion extends to those who are suffering the greatest degree of deprivation. Australia's humanitarian migration quota should be filled by those most lacking in the resources and opportunities that are a pre-condition to human survival and flourishing.

This would not preclude any 'existing refugees' from applying for asylum, but they would have to battle in the destitution stakes for a visa against a far greater number of often more needy people.

The other part of the solution requires us to disqualify asylum seekers who come by boat from refugee eligibility. There are two imperatives driving this. The first is pragmatic. We should not encourage or reward uncontrollable risk. Paternalism is justified where the activity involves a grave risk to the individual.

Asylum seekers have no control over the seaworthiness of their vessel and no remedy if things go wrong. There is no safe way to come to Australia by boat. These people, and their children, need to be saved from themselves.

The second reason is principled. As noted above, Australian has a strict annual cap on humanitarian arrivals. Each boat arrival by an impatient, relatively well-off (by displaced person standards) asylum-seeker reduces the opportunity for any of the other 15 million refugees patiently waiting off-shore to come to our opulent shores. More than half of these people have waited more than 10 years to be granted asylum.

While there is no queue in which these 15 million people are assembled, there are Australian migration places which they can potentially fill. Their prospects are becoming virtually hopeless by the increasing number of illegal arrivals coming to Australia.

Australia is uniquely placed in relation to its refugee intake. We are an island. There is no safe way to get here. We do not have any refugee producing neighbours. We are entitled and should refuse refugee eligibility to any person who appears on our shores unannounced.

This leaves the difficult situation of what to do with asylum-seekers who come by aeroplane. Principle dictates that they too must be prohibited from applying for refugee status, save for the exceptional case where a change to their personal circumstances or the social and political landscape in their country since their arrival makes them a refugee. These claims are already part of our existing law and the numbers are negligible.

Australia should also increase its intake of displaced people to say double the current annual quota of 13,750 humanitarian visas. If all these people are processed offshore it would still be a net financial gain to Australia. In the 2011-12 year it is projected that the refugee determination process will cost approximately $1 billion. It costs nearly $100,000 to process each asylum seeker, making Australia's refugee determination process the most expensive on earth. The additional cost of settling the larger number of displaced people would be a fraction of the current cost of the misery that is the refugee industry.

Ideally, Australia should absorb even more than the estimated 25,000 displaced people annually. But for any policy to work, it needs to be politically sellable. A doubling of current numbers would be politically controversial, but the community would support it given the immense benefits in the form of bringing to an end the current calamitous refugee picture.

It may seem cruel to send people to their country of origin who come to Australia without prior refugee recognition. But once the policy that Australia only takes refugees who are offshore is promulgated, those in search of refugee settlement will not come to Australia. As noted above, these arrivals are strategic travelers who make informed decisions about where they prefer to resettle. Shutting the door to illegal entrants to Australia means these people will simply change their travel plans, in the same way they did during the John Howard era, when the number of unauthorised boat arrivals dwindled to nearly zero.

Moreover, the moral worth of all people is identical. The ostensible cruelty that would be associated with sending a small number of illegal arrivals to their homeland would be overwhelmed by the compassion surge associated with abolishing mandatory detention and giving the most destitute people in the world a chance to flourish in Australia, especially if the number of humanitarian visas is greatly increased.

In a nutshell, the world would be a far improved place if the 2011 humanitarian intake for Australia was filled by the first 13,750 people in famine ravaged Somalia who are cleared of having a serious infectious disease were put on a plane and settled in Australia. In the destitution stakes they are the most desperate people on earth. If we do not accept them into Australia many will die. On a scale of need, their's could not be higher. As matters currently stand, none of these people will arrive in Australia. Their spots will mainly be taken by people with the resources to come to Australia from Iran or Afghanistan.

Conclusion

The Refugee Convention leads to unjust outcomes. It has a humanitarian overtone, but is devoid of an overarching justification. Its greatest failing is that it prioritises relatively minor interests such as the right to protect one's political opinion over basic human needs. The fact that an applicant's cause of distress must be linked to the specific grounds in the definition – that is, persecution due to race, religion, nationality, membership of a particular social group or political opinion – renders the Convention unnecessarily and unjustly restrictive. It bars people whose lives are unbearable because of war, famines, drought and earthquakes from receiving protection under the Convention. The current definition ignores the human interests that are most essential for survival. In light of this, it is time to reform the definition of a refugee so that Australia's collective compassion is targeted more directly at those who are suffering the greatest degree of deprivation.

The world has changed markedly since the mid 20th century. Regrettably, the main international law document for resettling the needy has not. For the past three decades mass people movement and suffering is most likely to be the result of famine, natural disasters and wars as opposed to people suffering owing to their race, religion or political preferences.

Moreover, it is absurd that Australia should only provide for migration to our shores for humanitarian reasons for people who manage to escape their homeland – often the most destitute people and those lives are most at risk are those who have no mobility to leave their homeland.

The only manner in which Australia can implement a fair, coherent and efficient refugee policy is if we select our refugees, not allow them to select us. At the same time we need to take in more refugees.

Australia needs either to withdraw from the Convention or to observe only its 'spirit'. The world would be a much better place if Australia prioritised humane outcomes over worshipping outdated legal instruments: it would mean an end to mandatory detention and drownings near our shores and ensure that priority in refugee determinations was given to the most needy (not the most pushy).

13
Shrewd politics of tax and transfer

Sinclair Davidson

Shrewd politics

Milton Friedman has described introduction of the welfare state in Germany in the 1880s as a combination of paternalism and shrewd politics.[1] During the last 130 years the welfare state has grown very substantially across western Europe and its offshoots in the new world. That growth in government is now widely recognised has having imposed huge fiscal costs and social problems in many of those societies – as Margaret Thatcher has long recognised.

Welfare benefits, distributed with little or no consideration of their effects on behaviour, encouraged illegitimacy, facilitated the breakdown of families, and replaced incentives favouring work and self-reliance with perverse encouragement for idleness and cheating. [2]

While the shrewd politics has remained, paternalism as the underlying rationale for welfare has changed. Now there is an argument for 'egalitarianism' or 'equity' underpinning welfare. The apparently adverse consequences of inequality have most recently been set out in *The Spirit Level* by Richard Wilkinson and Kate Pickett.[3] Their conclusion is that society would be better off with higher levels of equality rather than lower levels of equality. To be sure, at some extreme levels of inequality this must be true – yet their argument related to the levels of inequality that are experienced in a sub-set of OECD countries.[4]

The solutions usually offered to 'problems of inequality' are for high levels of progressive taxation – a research report prepared for the

1 Milton and Rose Friedman, *Free to Choose: A Personal Statement*. Penguin Books, 1980, 125.
2 Margaret Thatcher, *The Downing Street Years*. HarperCollins, 1993, 8.
3 Richard Wilkinson and Kate Pickett, *The Spirit Level: Why More Equal Societies Almost Always Do Better*. Allen Lane, 2009.
4 For a comprehensive critique of Wilkinson and Pickett see Peter Saunders, 'When Prophecy Fails.' The Centre for Independent Studies, 2011 (and chapter three of this volume).

Australian Council of Trade Unions argues, 'Progressive taxation is a key policy mechanism for addressing wealth inequality' – high levels of government spending, and labour market intervention.[5] As Terry Carney and Peter Hanks indicate, the fiscal costs of these 'solutions' are substantial so government has also undertaken 'more preventive and more targeted measures'.[6] Means-tested welfare has problems of its own and the preventive measures have resulted in an expansion of the state.

Carney and Hanks trace differing attitudes towards egalitarianism.[7] Classical liberals, they argue, view poverty as a product of personal choice and poor government policy. The solutions to poverty involve personal charity and increased economic growth. Another group, described as 'true conservatives', believe that inequality arises from innate cultural diversity or rewards, 'elite' performance, and responses – not solutions – entail reinforcing societal institutions such as the family, church, and other voluntary community groups. These views, it must be said, are now largely in the minority. The dominant view, at least amongst elite opinion, is that 'inequality is a product of market failure, discrimination, [and] historical imbalances in the distribution of property.'[8] Peter Saunders, however, points to the puzzle that welfare spending has increased faster than has economic growth.[9] By definition, one might expect that the need for welfare would decline as the economy grew.

In order to provide insight into the growth of welfare spending, I collected data from the Australian Bureau of Statistics and annual Budget Papers on government spending. Four areas of government spending can be classified as being 'welfare' – Education, Health, Social Security and Welfare, and Housing and Community Development. These four items made up some 58.3 percent of government spending in 2000-01 and increased to 62.3 percent in 2008-09 before declining to 59.1 percent in 2011-12. That represents an increase from $104 billion in

5 David Neal, Cassandra Govan, Mike Norton, and Dan Ariely, *Australian Attitudes Towards Wealth Inequality and Progressive Taxation*. A report prepared for the ACTU, 2011.
6 Terry Carney and Peter Hanks, *Social Security in Australia*. Oxford University Press, 1994, 2.
7 Carny and Hanks, 1994, 1-2.
8 Carny and Hanks, 1994, 2.
9 Peter Saunders, *Australia's Welfare Habit and How To Kick It*. Duffy and Snellgrove, 2004, 4-6.

2000-01 to $216 billion in 2011-12.[10] At the same time the participation rate in the labour force has increased, while unemployment has fallen, and average weekly earnings increased. Even a stricter definition of welfare just to include the budget item, 'Social Security and Welfare', shows massive growth from $66.9 billion to $121.9 billion during the past 11 years – that is, an increase of 82 percent.

The tax and spend aspects of the welfare state are highly wasteful and cannot be said to have been successful. As Friedman wrote more than 30 years ago, 'The repeated failure of well-intentioned programs is not an accident. It is not simply the result of mistakes of execution. The failure is deeply rooted in the use of bad means to achieve good objectives.'[11] Friedrich von Hayek is less tolerant; he describes any policy that aims to promote equality as 'a wholly illusory ideal, and any attempt concretely to realize it apt to produce a nightmare.'[12] He makes the very important point that it is not intentions that matter but rather in 'doing what in fact most benefits others'.[13]

Australian egalitarianism and progressive taxation

Fred Argy defines *economic* egalitarianism as creating a welfare safety net, widely sharing the gains from productivity improvements, addressing the structural causes of inequality and proving a 'voice' for workers. He also talks about sacrifices being distributed by the 'ability to bear'.[14] This is a somewhat pragmatic definition of egalitarianism and cannot be described as being in the Rawlsian tradition.[15] Argy argues, for example, that complete equality is 'neither achievable nor desirable', not because the economic costs are prohibitive, but because people are inherently different. If people do have such very different skills and interests and risk tolerance and the like, it is not clear why equality is a

---

10 The $104 billion would be $134 billion in 2010 dollars.
11 Milton and Rose Friedman, 1980, 124.
12 Friedrich von Hayek, *The Mirage of Social Justice: Law, Legislation and Liberty.* The University of Chicago Press, volume 2, 1976, 85.
13 Hayek, 1976, 72.
14 Fred Argy, *Where To From Here? Australian Egalitarianism Under Threat.* Allen & Unwin, 2003, 166.
15 Rawls argues that inequality can only be tolerated to the extent that it benefits the least advantaged in society.

desirable outcome at all. In other words, policies that promote equality are in search of a justification.

Despite this lack of principle Australia maintains a highly progressive tax system and redistributes a substantial amount of income from high-income earners to middle and low-income earners.[16] The Australian Council of Trade Unions would like to increase the level of progressivity in the tax system: 'Sixty percent of Australians support raising taxes for higher income earners and the same proportion want lower taxes for middle income earners, according to new research commissioned by trade unions'.[17]

The difficulty with this particular argument is that the Australian tax system is already very progressive. In August 2007, then Treasurer Peter Costello made the claim that 'something like 60 percent of Australian families are paying no net tax. That is, their family tax benefits are outweighing their tax liabilities and that's something that's actually really helped Australian families.'[18] In a careful analysis, Peter Whiteford compares cash transfers and the direct tax burden and reports that the poorest quintile received 'more than 30 times as much in cash transfers as they paid in direct taxes' in 2005 – that figure was down from over 55 times in 2000.[19]

What is clear is that the personal income tax burden is highly progressive. Each year the Australian Taxation Office releases statistical information relating to the tax system. The data is released with a lag and the 2008-09 financial year is the latest available. Using those statistics it is possible to determine the individual tax burden by income level.

---

16 Peter Whiteford suggests that almost 50 percent of Australian government spending can be described as social spending. See Peter Whiteford, 'The Australian Tax-Transfer System: Architecture and Outcomes.' *The Economic Record*. 86, 2010, 528. As shown above, however, that figure is under-estimated.
17 Sabra Lane, 2011, 'ACTU Pushes For Tax Reform.' *ABC News*. August 29 2011.
18 *The 7.30 Report*, 'Peter Costello Talks About The Latest Interest Rate Rise.' August 8 2007.
19 Whiteford, 2010, 532.

Figure 1. Individual income tax burden

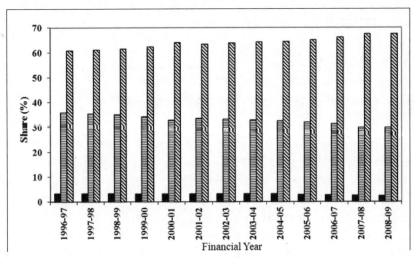

Source: ATO Tax Statistics, author calculations.

By collecting data from the Australian Taxation Office (ATO) and arbitrarily segmenting it into three segments – the bottom twenty-five percent; the middle fifty percent; and the top twenty-five percent – and calculating how much net tax they pay, it is very clear that the tax burden has increased for the top end of the income distribution. The top twenty-five percent of taxpayers paid 67 percent of net personal income tax in 2008-09. The bottom twenty-five percent paid just 2.4 percent. It is possible to refine the data further; the top five percent of taxpayers paid 33.7 percent of net income tax in 2008-09, with an (average) effective tax rate of 42.2 percent.

That is how a progressive income tax system is meant to operate. High income earners are meant to pay more income tax than do low income earners, and in that regard the Australian tax system works as it was designed to work.

It could be argued that the income tax system is highly progressive in order to compensate for regressive indirect taxation so that the overall net effect of the tax system is roughly proportional. That proposition, however, is purely empirical. Once sin taxes (taxes of alcohol and tobacco) are removed from the equation it is clear that the Australian tax system is highly progressive even after accounting for indirect taxation.[20] In a 2008 analysis into inequality, the OECD found that Australia and the United States have the most progressive tax systems in the OECD, collecting 'the most tax from people in the top decile relative to the share of market income that they earn.'[21]

How does progressive taxation benefit the poor?

Whiteford makes the point that the inter-relationship between tax and welfare has long been recognised in Australia. In particular, taxation is how the welfare state is financed and welfare spending constitutes the bulk of government spending.[22] To the extent that a progressive tax system raised more revenue than, say, a proportional tax system, then it would be clear how progressive taxation benefited the poor. This would come at the expense of high-income earners, so we would also have to take the costs of raising revenue via a progressive tax into account but, in principle, the case could be made.

Figure two shows the distribution of the share of taxable income and the distribution of the share of net income tax paid by income quantiles for 2008-09. As can be seen, taxpayers below the 80th percentile pay a lower share of net income tax than their share of taxable income; taxpayers above the 80th percentile pay more in net income tax than their share of taxable income. The 80th percentile, is well above average earnings. In other words, a progressive income tax does not only favour the poor; it also favours middle income earners who pay less tax than they would under a proportional tax system.

20 Sinclair Davidson, 2004, 'Taxation With Misrepresentation: Australia's Revenue Lobby In Denial.' *Policy*. CIS, 20(4), 31-37.
21 OECD, *Growing Unequal: Income Distribution And Poverty In OECD Countries*. 2008, 106.
22 Whiteford, 2010, 528.

Figure 2. Distribution of taxable income and net tax (2008-09)

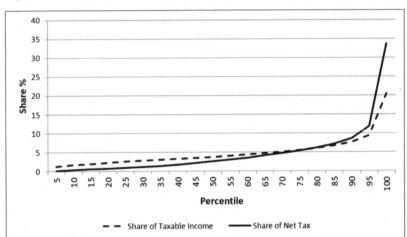

ATO Tax Statistics.

The American economist, Deirdre McCloskey, specifically argues that the policy of taxing the rich so that the poor might prosper has failed. She gives two reasons why that is so. First, following Robert Nozick, taxation is a form of slavery and is associated with various economic costs.[23] She also argues that most social spending is not designed to benefit the poor, but rather the middle class. She illustrates this point by means of a back of the envelope calculation. The US Government collects about 25 percent of US GDP in taxation; if a third of that amount were distributed to the 34 million Americans described as being 'poor', then each one would receive about US$30,000. A family of four – two parents and two children – would have a combined income of US$120,000 and could hardly be described as being 'poor' with that level of income. She concludes by observing, 'So it must not be true that the government's taxes go mainly, or even much at all, to the poor.'[24]

It is possible to replicate that thought experiment in Australia.

---

23 These costs are described in Alex Robson, 'How High Taxation Makes us Poorer.' In Peter Saunders (editor), *Taxploitation: The Case for Income Tax Reform*. CIS, 2006.
24 Deirdre McCloskey, *The Bourgeois Virtues: Ethics For An Age Of Commerce*. The University of Chicago Press, 2006, 43-46.

According to the Budget Papers the Commonwealth Government intends to spend \$121.9 billion in the 2011-12 financial year on Social Security and Welfare. That sum of money – 33.3 percent of the Commonwealth budget – does not include health, education or housing – items that also constitute welfare spending. Making the assumption that there could be as many as two and a half million poor Australians, that level of expenditure would be enough to transfer over \$48 000 to each of them. Even if we considered that the government should distribute money to the bottom twenty percent of Australians, that would still amount to over \$29 000 each.

This is a practical illustration of something economists call Director's law. This is the notion that government spending is primarily designed to benefit the middle class or middle income earners. The consequence of government spending money on middle income earners is 'tax-welfare churn' or middle-class welfare. Peter Saunders describes this situation as 'many households find themselves paying money into the system only to get it straight back again in the form of government payments and services.'[25]

One particular problem associated with churn over and above the pure waste and inefficiency is the existence of high so-called effective marginal tax rates. Much of the Australian welfare system is means tested. As the income of individuals rises, so they lose welfare benefits. The interaction between higher rates of taxation and lower welfare benefits means that work incentives are undermined.

Many recipients may not view middle class welfare as welfare per se. Former Prime Minister John Howard told the American Enterprise Institute in 2008 that, 'The taxation system should generously recognise the cost of raising children. This is not middle class welfare. It is merely a taxation system with some semblance of social vision.'[26] The difficulty with this particular argument is that any social vision somehow exempts government spending from being welfare.

Saunders makes the argument that everyone is paying for everyone

---

25 Peter Saunders, *The Government Giveth and The Government Taketh Away: Tax-Welfare Churning and The Case For Welfare State Opt-Outs*. The Centre for Independent Studies, 2007, 23.
26 John Howard, 'Keeping Faith with our Common Values.' The 2008 Irving Kristol Lecture. American Enterprise Institute, 2008.

else's welfare 'but few of us seem to be aware of it.'[27] That could be true; voters could be under a fiscal illusion that allows them to think that they are getting a bargain from the government.[28] To the extent that middle income earners pay less of the tax share and receive relatively more of the government spending share they are getting a bargain. On the other hand, government policy in a democracy is determined by the median voter and, as McCloskey tells us, the median voter 'is not enthusiastic about helping the poor.'[29] Following McCloskey, it is important to realise that this churn is a feature of our democracy, not a bug in the welfare system.

What can be done?

It is only through an understanding that the expansion of the welfare system benefits the median voter and not the poor per se that we can appreciate why the welfare system continues to expand. The massive welfare system and the progressive income tax exist to redistribute income to the middle class. As Hayek as argued, 'Much of what is today done in the name of "social justice" is thus not only unjust but also unsocial in the true sense of the word: it amounts simply to the protection of entrenched interests.'[30] Unfortunately, that 'entrenched interest' is the median voter in a democracy; in other words, the status quo has majoritarian support. This makes it much harder to unwind the welfare state.

Proposals to unwind the welfare state usually involve tightening up the conditions for redistribution, while Saunders has proposed an opt-out feature.[31] Given the democratic demand for welfare, it is not clear that either of these approaches would gain wide-spread support. Rather the costs and failures of the welfare system should be emphasised. It

---

27 Saunders, 2007, 5.
28 Fiscal illusion is a set of strategies that the state adopts in the hope of altering voters' fiscal consciousness. In particular the state hopes to convince voters that the tax burden is not nearly as onerous as it is, while the benefits of public spending are greater than they are. See Sinclair Davidson, 2011, 'Fiscal Illusion: How Big Government Makes Tax Look Small.' In Robert Carling (editor), *Taxploitation II: Tax Reform for Incentive, Productivity and Economic Growth.* The Centre for Independent Studies, 2011.
29 McCloskey, 2006, 46.
30 Hayek, 2006, 96.
31 Saunders, 2007, chapter 5.

is important to remember that fiscal illusion plays an important part in the demand for welfare. For as long as voters have the perception that welfare is a value proposition, it is unsurprising that welfare expands beyond the provision of a safety net for those individuals in actual need.

It is quite clear that the welfare system does not promote egalitarianism and that Australians are not egalitarian per se. Saunders has shown that Australians value a 'fair go' and are meritocratic but that is a long way from supporting massive income redistribution.[32] That suggests that greed and self-interest can be harnessed to drive welfare reform. If the costs associated with churn were emphasised it is quite possible that meaningful reform could occur. Rather than tighten welfare eligibility, and so increase effective marginal tax rates, tax rates themselves could be lowered. This would increase the returns to work and lift many individuals out of the tax churn system. Other reforms such as providing tax deductions for school fees rather than funding schools themselves would provide an incentive for parents to invest in their children's education and make the education system responsive to parents rather than bureaucrats.

Making the costs of the welfare system highly transparent would go a long way to reducing those costs over time. On the other hand, however, if the electorate chooses to bear the costs of the welfare system even after those costs become transparent then, at least, an honest choice will have been made.

Conclusion

The provision of 'social justice' via the welfare system remains shrewd politics. It provides for a massive redistribution while doing little for the actual poor. The poor do get some benefit from the welfare but not nearly as much as we might imagine. At a time of economic prosperity and continued economic growth, the amount of welfare should be declining, yet we see massive growth.

An insatiable growth in the welfare system via demands for 'social justice' is inconsistent with prosperity in the long-run. While nobody

---

32 Saunders, 2004, 75-78.

should begrudge a genuine safety net for people in actual need, it should not come as a surprise that the last ten years have seen a decline in productivity just as the welfare state has expanded faster than economic growth. Ultimately the best guarantor of prosperity for all is a prosperous economy.

Contributors

Wesley Aird

Wesley Aird spends most of his working life solving problems so that indigenous Australians can become genuine participants in the real economy. His primary work is with resource sector companies in the development of initiatives for Indigenous employment, training and business. Wesley is an applicant on the Gold Coast Native Title Claim and is the business manager of a company wholly owned by the Gold Coast Native Title Group which involves management of projects relating to cultural heritage, native title and community development.

He was a member of the National Indigenous Council during the last term of the Howard Government. For more than a decade Wesley has been a project manager and advisor in the resource sector. Before that he served in the military for 10 years and was the first Indigenous graduate from the Royal Military College, Duntroon.

Mirko Bagaric

Professor Mirko Bagaric is a professor of law at the Deakin Law School. A former member of the Migration and Refugee Review Tribunals, he is co-author of Migration and Refugee Law (Cambridge University Press). He has written more than 20 books on legal and moral issues.

Terry Barnes

Terry Barnes was senior personal adviser to two federal health ministers, Michael Wooldridge and Tony Abbott. He oversaw the Commonwealth's funding responsibilities under the Australian Health Care Agreements at the Victorian Department of Premier and Cabinet. He had an advisory role in negotiating the 2003-08 Health Care Agreements on behalf of Victoria.

He conducted the National Competition Policy Review of Pharmacy Legislation in 1999 and drafted the Wilkinson Report. He worked as interim chief of staff to the Community Services and Housing ministers in the Baillieu Victorian government.

Grace Collier

Grace Collier was employed in the union movement for many years before working for employer organisations. In 2003, she formed *Industrial Relations Consulting*. The business specializes in staff performance management and dismissals, collective agreement making, restructuring, industrial relations strategy, union relationship management, and financial rescues.

Her articles on industrial relations matters have appeared in various publications including the *The Australian*, *The Australian Financial Review*, *IPA Review*. She was a contributor to *The Greens: Policies, Realities and Consequences* 2011.

Sinclair Davidson

Professor Sinclair Davidson is Professor of Institutional Economics at RMIT University and a Senior Fellow at the Institute of Public Affairs. His opinion pieces have been published in *The Age*, *The Australian*, *The Australian Financial Review*, *The Sydney Morning Herald*, and *The Wall Street Journal Asia*.

Gary Johns

The Honourable Dr Gary Johns is an Associate Professor of Public Policy at the Australian Catholic University. He served in the Keating Labor Government and, later, as an Associate Commissioner of the Commonwealth Productivity Commission. He was a Senior Fellow of the Institute of Public Affairs, and a senior consultant with ACIL Tasman economic consultants.

He received the Centenary Medal and the Fulbright Professional Award in Australian-United States Alliance Studies. He is a member of the editorial board of *Agenda* (ANU) and a columnist for *The Australian* newspaper. He is author of, among other publications, *Aboriginal Self-Determination: The Whiteman's Dream* 2011.

Asher Judah

Asher Judah is a Research Fellow at the Institute of Public Affairs. He is formerly a manager of policy and communications at the Master Builders Association of Victoria, and an economics, education and livestock adviser at the Victorian Farmers Federation. He is also an active member of the Australia India Business Council.

Ruth Limkin

Pastor Ruth Limkin works as the CEO of a Brisbane charity, and a pastor, working with young adults. In 2008, she was awarded the Margaret Dooley Award for social justice and human rights writing. She has a Bachelor of Business, majoring in Management and Leadership, and is a lifelong student of leadership, innovation and strategic thinking.

She is a contributor with *The Courier-Mail* and she blogs at breadandjustice.com

Julie Novak

Julie Novak is a Research Fellow at the Institute of Public Affairs, and a PhD candidate in the School of Economics, Finance and Marketing, RMIT University. She was a researcher at the Productivity Commission.

She has contributed to three books, including *The National Curriculum: A Critique*, is a regular blogger, including on the prominent Catallaxy website, and contributes frequently to major Australian newspapers.

Jeremy Sammut

Dr Jeremy Sammut is a research fellow at The Centre for Independent Studies. He has a BA (Hons) from Macquarie University and PhD in Australian political and social history from Monash University.

He is the author of *Fatally Flawed: The Child Protection Crisis in Australia* (2009), *The Power and the Responsibility: Child Protection in the Post-Welfare State Era* (2010) and *Do Not Damage and Disturb: On Child Protection Failures and the Pressure on Out of Home Care in Australia (2011).*

Peter Saunders

Professor Peter Saunders is Professor Emeritus of Sociology, University of Sussex, England. He is a Distinguished Fellow of the Centre for Independent Studies, Australia, and Professorial Research Fellow at Civitas, London.

Peter Urban

Peter Urban worked in the Bureau of Agricultural Economics and was Chief Economist at the Department of Foreign Affairs and Trade.

Since leaving DFAT, he has worked as a senior analyst with the Commonwealth Grants Commission, a consulting economist and policy adviser and written frequently about domestic and international economic policy issues for *The Australian Financial Review*, *The Australian* and *The Canberra Times*.

Cassandra Wilkinson

Cassandra Wilkinson was a Labor Ministerial adviser and a Director in the NSW public service specialising in public transport. She subsequently worked as a Director within the economics practice of Deloitte Touche Tohmatsu before joining the staff of NSW Premier Kristina Keneally.

In 2011, she joined Social Finance Pty Ltd to develop the use of Social Impact Bonds as a financing mechanism for bringing additional resources to the social sector. She is the author of *Don't Panic Nearly Everything is Better than You Think* and is a columnist for *The Australian*.